10 Mindframes for Visible Learning

The original Visible Learning research concluded that one of the most important influences on student achievement is how teachers think about learning and their own role. In *10 Mindframes for Visible Learning*, John Hattie and Klaus Zierer define the ten behaviors or mindframes that teachers need to adopt in order to maximize student success. These include:

- thinking of and evaluating your impact on students' learning;
- the importance of assessment and feedback for teachers;
- working collaboratively and the sense of community;
- the notion that learning needs to be challenging;
- engaging in dialogue and the correct balance between talking and listening;
- conveying the success criteria to learners;
- building positive relationships.

These powerful mindframes, which should underpin every action in schools, are founded on the principle that teachers are evaluators, change agents, learning experts, and seekers of feedback who are constantly engaged with dialogue and challenge.

This practical guide, which includes questionnaires, scenarios, checklists, and exercises, will show any school exactly how to implement Hattie's mindframes to maximize success.

John Hattie is Professor, Deputy Dean, and Director of the Melbourne Education Research Institute at the University of Melbourne, Australia. He is Chair of the Board of the Australian Institute for Teaching and School Leadership, and Associate Director of the ARC-Science of Learning Research Centre.

Klaus Zierer is Professor of Education at the University of Augsburg, Germany, and Associate Research Fellow of the ESRC-funded Centre on Skills, Knowledge and Organisational Performance (SKOPE) at the University of Oxford UK.

D0646140

CORWIN

Ready to put Professor Hattie's research into practice?

John Hattie's powerful research forms the basis of Visible Learning[plus], a proven process for collecting and analyzing evidence to help educators understand their impact and make strategic decisions to deliver the best possible outcomes for students.

Corwin is the exclusive provider of Visible Learning[plus] seminars, institutes, and consulting in the United States, Canada, and Australia. For over 25 years, our mission of "helping educators make the greatest impact" has guided us in finding practical, research-based solutions to the challenges that educators face.

Learn more at www.corwin.com/visiblelearning.

Corwin, a SAGE Company
2455 Teller Road
Thousand Oaks, CA 91320
Tel: 800-233-9936
Fax: 800-417-2466
sales@corwin.com

10 Mindframes for Visible Learning

Teaching for Success

John Hattie and
Klaus Zierer

Routledge
Taylor & Francis Group

LONDON AND NEW YORK

First published 2018
by Routledge
2 Park Square, Milton Park, Abingdon, Oxon OX14 4RN

and by Routledge
711 Third Avenue, New York, NY 10017

Routledge is an imprint of the Taylor & Francis Group, an informa business

© 2018 John Hattie and Klaus Zierer

British Library Cataloguing-in-Publication Data
A catalogue record for this book is available from the British Library

Library of Congress Cataloging-in-Publication Data
A catalog record for this book has been requested

ISBN: 978-1-5443-2567-5 (pbk)

Typeset in Bembo and Helvetica Neue
by Apex CoVantage, LLC

Contents

Figures

Preface

How we *think* about the *impact* of what we do is more important than *what* we do

15,000 hours with 50 teachers

We all spend around 15,000 hours of our lives at school (cf. Rutter et al., 1980) and are taught by roughly 50 different teachers in this time. When we try to remember these teachers who had a positive impact on us, we can often recall only a few. Some were good, and some were bad. In both cases, we sometimes remember their names and perhaps their clothing or a few of their typical mannerisms. Although we can count the teachers who "changed" us on the fingers of one hand, we would perhaps need to grow a few extra hands to count the latter in the same way. Be that as it may, the good news about this memory is that almost every one of us did end up having a good teacher or two. The bad news is that the vast majority of the teachers we had in school have been erased from our memory entirely. We know neither their names nor the subject they taught nor anything else.

How can it be that some teachers succeed in remaining in our memory for years or even decades, whereas others fade into oblivion after just a brief period of time?

Let us take a closer look at our memories of good teachers: What do you recollect when you think about them? When we surveyed many adults with this question, there were two major answers: they recalled the teachers who tried to turn you onto the teacher's passion, or they recalled the teachers who saw something in you that you may not have seen in yourself, or both. It was their ways of thinking, their ways of supporting, their ways of challenging, and their ways of passion that you are most likely to recall. It is unlikely to be because they taught a particular subject or were friendly or not, but because they had an impact on you.

This book is about just these teachers, the ones who have remained in our memories in a positive light over the course of years or even decades. They were teachers who had a major impact on our learning and on our education – and oftentimes the effect of this impact is still with us today. The main focus in this book is on taking a closer look at the core notions of why they had this impact.

Simon Sinek and the Golden Circle

There are clear parallels between educational expertise and successful leadership. The task in both cases is to challenge and encourage people to the greatest possible extent in their development, in their thinking, and in their actions. In 2009, the American motivator and writer Simon Sinek held a TED Talk titled "How Great Leaders Inspire Action." This talk gave rise to global discussions within a short period of time and is still the third most viewed film on TED. com today – with more than 20 million views in the past six years. Shortly afterwards, Simon Sinek published the book *Start with Why* (2009), in which he fleshed out the idea first expounded in his talk.

At first glance, his idea seems too simple to be true: How are three concentric circles labeled with the words "what," "how," and "why" supposed to explain success? Only upon closer examination do the connections these circles represent prove to be helpful in describing successful leadership. And they can also help us to better understand educational expertise.

Simon Sinek argues that leadership can be considered from three different perspectives: First, it can be seen from the perspective of *what* successful leaders do. Second, we can take the approach of asking *how* leaders do what they do. And third, we can ask ourselves *why* leaders do what they do. To illustrate this concept, Simon Sinek uses the drawing found in Figure 0.1, which he calls the Golden Circle (cf. Sinek, 2009).

The main message of Simon Sinek's concept is that average leaders start and finish their thinking at the outermost circle. They ask themselves what they are doing and usually do not think any further. And so, they fail to consider the much more important questions of

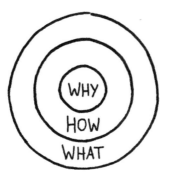

FIGURE 0.1 The Golden Circle

how and why they are doing what they are doing. In this way, average leaders often lose sight of their actual goal and thus also fail at their main task; namely, that of challenging and encouraging people to the greatest possible extent in their development, in their thinking, and in their actions. The response in those following the leader is a hollow, mechanical reaction to external stimuli; they are incapable of acting out of an inner conviction. They just do the job, take the actions, and run their schools irrespective of the impact on their students.

Successful leaders take a different approach. For them, the main question is why something should be done. This leads them to the question of how to do something and finally to that of what to do. Simon Sinek brings his argument to the point with the following statement: The important thing for successful leaders is not what they do; much more important is how and why they do what they do. Hence, he sees the secret of success in beginning with the inner circle and the question of why and then continuing outward from there by asking the questions of how and what. Simon Sinek presents three examples to illustrate his concept: Apple, Martin Luther King Jr, and the Wright brothers.

What is the secret of Apple's success? It surely has nothing to do with what Apple does: Apple makes computers, tablets, and cell phones – as do many other companies. Besides, if we take a closer look at these devices, we have to admit that they are not much better than those of the competition – a smartphone that bends in your pocket might be a unique feature but certainly not in a positive sense. Neither can it have anything to do with how Apple does what it does. Rather, if we take a detailed look at the company's record on this point we see exactly the opposite: low wages, high environmental impact, and poor working conditions. Thus, the secret of Apple's success must lie in the question of why: People who buy an Apple product today do not get just a technical device. They also get a personal philosophy, a way of life, and a passion to boot. Apple stands for the feeling of living a better life.

Why is Martin Luther King Jr among the most well-known and influential leaders of the African American civil rights movement? Surely not just because of what he did. He was not the only humanist of his time, and his ideas were the ideas of a larger group of activists. Neither does it lie in how he did what he did. He was doubtlessly a brilliant and passionate orator, but even that was not the key thing that set him apart from his fellow activists. It is thus necessary to look for the reason for the success of Martin Luther King Jr elsewhere: Why did he do what he did? The 250,000 people who participated in the March on Washington on August 28, 1963, had not received an invitation. They came because they believed in Martin Luther King Jr – less in what he said or in how he said it than in why he said it. Martin Luther King Jr had a vision of why he was doing what he was doing. "I have a dream" are his immortal words – not "I have a plan." The people who heard Martin Luther King Jr on this day were deeply moved, shared the same values, and had a common vision. They all believed that this day would change everything.

On December 17, 1903, the Wright brothers became the first people to fly a powered aircraft. Why they? Compared with other teams with the same goal, their prospects were very poor: no funding, no support from the government, no connections to powerful people, and no special education. Samuel Pierpont Langley, their most well-known rival in the race to be crowned as pioneer of flight, enjoyed all the advantages the Wright brothers lacked: funding, cooperation with the government, excellent contacts, and even a professorship at the United States Naval Academy. So why the Wright brothers? Both teams were highly motivated, both teams had a clear goal in sight, and both teams worked hard to achieve it. The difference was neither luck nor a favorable turn of events. It was inspiration: Whereas Langley's team wanted to be the first to gain fame and honor, the Wright brothers were driven by the vision, the belief in the dream of flying. Langley's team was motivated by what they aimed to do, whereas the Wright brothers were focused on the question of why they were doing it.

To recapitulate, the success of Apple, Martin Luther King Jr, and the Wright brothers illustrates Simon Sinek's main message: They all began not with the question of what they wanted to do but that of why they wanted to do something. They all had a vision, a passion, a belief – and they were all capable of communicating them and sharing them with others.

As with educators, it is their vision, their passion, their belief that they can and do enhance the learning lives of their students. This is the core "why" educators do what they do. A major theme in this book is to explore the ways educators think about their work, and if nothing else, we want to move the debate from how we best teach, to how we best evaluate the impact of this teaching. The latter goes more directly to the heart of educators' success and reason for being in schools, and benefits students the most.

Howard Gardner and the 3 Es

It is surprising and fascinating that the message Simon Sinek developed on the basis of experience and expertise agrees with an empirical finding: Howard Gardner initiated the "Good Work Project" (2005) together with Mihály Csíkszentmihályi and William Damon in 1995. The aim was to answer the question of what makes up successful work. The three researchers conducted more than 1,200 interviews with people from nine different occupational fields to determine how professional success in these fields is defined and how it is possible to identify good work in them. Their analysis of the extensive dataset boils down to a seemingly simple formula: Good work is characterized by 3 Es. It consists in a combination and synthesis of excellence, engagement, and ethics. A successful worker knows what she is doing, sees to it that she gets it done, and can name reasons for why she is doing what she is doing. It does not matter whether one is discussing the work of a janitor or the work of a top manager: Good work is a question of excellence, engagement, and ethics.

To illustrate this notion, let us consider an example from daily life. Imagine the following situation: You order a cup of coffee at a bar. In the first case, the waiter communicates with you in a friendly and appreciative way while serving you your coffee, giving you the feeling that you are a welcome guest at the bar. In the second case, the waiter serves you the coffee without speaking with you or even looking at you, giving you the feeling of not being welcome. In both cases, you get your cup of coffee. So the result is the same, but the difference is in how the result was arrived at in the two cases, and this illustrates the main message of the 3 Es: Good work is not just a

FIGURE 0.2 The 3 Es

question of excellence, the knowledge and ability necessary to do the work, but also and especially a question of engagement, the motivation to do the work, and of ethics, the values and the reasons that are always connected with performing any kind of work.

Hence, the act of serving a cup of coffee can be of varying quality even though the cup of coffee we drink in the end is always the same. The quality depends vitally on the excellence, the engagement, and the ethics of the waiter. In terms of our discussion of Simon Sinek's concept of leadership, we might associate the excellence with the what, the engagement with the how, and the ethics with the why. It is, therefore, possible to combine Simon Sinek's concept with the empirical findings reached by Howard Gardner, Mihály Csíkszentmihályi, and William Damon. Again, we can illustrate this connection in the form of a simple circle (see Figure 0.2).

Educational expertise: competence and mindframes

The argument is that it is more about how teachers think about their tasks. It is more about the why do they do this rather than that in the moment-by-moment decision making in their classrooms (and in their staffrooms). This thinking is based on passion and enthusiasm to have an impact on students. This passion and enthusiasm manifests itself in the following set of ten mindframes. The first three relate to impact, the next two to change and challenge, and the last five to learning focus.

A. Impact

   1. I am an evaluator of my impact on student learning.

   2. I see assessment as informing my impact and next steps.

   3. I collaborate with my peers and my students about my conceptions of progress and my impact.

B. Change and Challenge

   4. I am a change agent and believe all students can improve.

   5. I strive for challenge and not merely "doing your best."

C. Learning Focus

   6. I give and help students understand feedback and I interpret and act on feedback given to me.

   7. I engage as much in dialogue as monologue.

   8. I explicitly inform students what successful impact looks like from the outset.

   9. I build relationships and trust so that learning can occur in a place where it is safe to make mistakes and learn from others.

   10. I focus on learning and the language of learning.

The distinguishing feature of these mindframes is that it is also possible to cite empirical evidence demonstrating that successful teachers behave the way they do on account of their mindframes. It is more about how they think about what they do that matters most, how they understand their impact, and their search for feedback to improve the positive impact they have on their students. In this way, mindframes can become visible. Thus, expert teachers have answers not only to the question of what they are doing but also to the questions of how and why they are doing what they are doing.

It is now clear how educational expertise is connected with the models proposed by Simon Sinek and Howard Gardner, Mihály Csíkszentmihályi, and William Damon: The key to successful behavior in school and instruction is not just knowledge and ability (in this sense, excellence and the question of what) but also will (in this sense, engagement and the question of how) and judgment (in this sense, ethics and the question of why). Particularly interesting is the fact that there is an inner link between these aspects: Ability is based on knowledge that can be retrieved only when there is a will to do so, and since there are always reasons for doing so, this will is based on judgment. In this sense, pedagogical activity is a deeply ethical activity. A teacher who can retrieve the necessary ability, knowledge, will, and judgment will act accordingly in a particular situation. And if the context is favorable, he or she will also be successful in this endeavor. If one of these aspects is missing, for instance the will, the teacher will, in all probability, fail. Figure 0.3 sums up this argument in the form of a model (ability, knowledge, will, judgment) (cf. Zierer, 2016a).

A high degree of competence alone is clearly not enough to lay the foundation for expertise, nor are even the best of mindframes. The important thing is rather the interaction between competence and mindframes. If we look at the biographies of typical teachers with this point in mind, we find that it is above all their mindframes that are susceptible to change throughout their careers: Although knowledge and ability remain relatively stable, will and judgment are put to the test each and every school day. It is ultimately teachers' mindframes that determine whether they are up to the challenging task of teaching successfully for their entire working lives.

FIGURE 0.3 ACAC model

Take a moment to consider against the background of our model why successful professionals suddenly experience burnout. It is certainly not due to a lack of competence. Rather, it is on account of shifts in their mindframes that formerly successful people no longer derive any pleasure or satisfaction from their work and, therefore, fail. A key reason for maintaining the mindframes we are outlining is the continual feeding of these mindframes with evidence of the impact that teachers have on students. It can be self-fulfilling.

It is also clear that it is much easier to foster competence than to change mindframes. But does this mean we should just give up? If we want to develop educational expertise, we have no choice other than to accept this challenge and make it into the main focus of teacher education and via the renewal of ongoing professional learning.

Successful teachers are passionate not only about the subject they teach but also about teaching and learning in general, about the learners, and about their profession. About their impact on their students. This passion is important not just for becoming a successful teacher but also for remaining in this challenging profession and, therefore, for remaining a successful teacher in the long term.

Why this book?

This book is the product of an examination of the Visible Learning meta-study (Hattie, 2013, 2014, 2015; Zierer, 2016b). We have both pored over the evidence provided in these sources, trying to make sense, make a story, and make interpretations as to why some interventions in schooling are much more impactful than others. We have debated, argued, and enjoyed trying to understand the core elements of success. Some have misleadingly used the rankings of influences in a narrow manner, preferring those at the top and ignoring those at the bottom of the rankings. Others have disliked the evidence as it did not fit with their own worldview. Others have said yes, but my class is different. Others have cherry-picked and promoted one influence over the other. Yes, maybe the first book could have been written to not lead to these misinterpretations. Although it was made clear that it was the overlapping of the many factors that led to the story, this point may not have been made sufficiently powerfully enough.

The search is for the core notions of what truly makes the difference between those who have high impact and those who have low impact on the learning lives of students. This is the purpose of this book. Certainly, it was clear that it was less the structures relating to schools and more the expertise of the educators that made the greatest differences. Certainly, students are marvelously variable and unique, but the simple message was that what worked best tended to work best with most students. The key, however, was not these notions – it was that educators had to be very mindful of their impact – the nature of what impact means, the magnitude of this impact, the worthwhileness of this impact.

All of the empirical evidence considered and applied to classroom practice in this book was taken from the Visible Learning meta-study. And the database continues to grow. In 2009, there were 800 meta-analyses, and now there are 1,400 and growing. The underlying story, however, has not changed; indeed, it has been reinforced by the addition of 600 meta-analyses. This book is less about repeating the story and more about searching for the core of what makes the greatest difference – and as we will see it comes directly to HOW educators think about their jobs, their interventions, their students, and their impact.

What is Visible Learning?

The work on the original Visible Learning meta-study took more than 15 to 20 years to complete. It involved analyzing more than 800 meta-analyses composing around 80,000 studies in which an estimated (because the number of test subjects is not always stated in the meta-analyses) 250 million learners took part – and, as just noted, the work on the Visible Learning project is not yet finished: A total of more than 1,400 meta-analyses now have been analyzed to date, but little has changed about the main messages of the study.

Only meta-analyses relating the achievement outcomes are considered. Others are doing similar work with respect to emotional and motivational outcomes (Korpershoek et al., 2016), how we teach (Hattie & Donoghue, 2016), and special education students (Mitchell, 2014), and it would be wonderful if there were meta-syntheses on retention to the last years of schooling, and physical and nutritional outcomes.

Visible Learning seeks to get to the crux of this multitude of findings from educational research and identify the main messages by synthesizing meta-analyses. The aim is to move from "what works" to "what works best" and when, for whom, and why. The search to understand these moderators (when, whom, why) was key in the search, and that there were so few moderators was quite surprising. The search involved first generating around 150 factors from the underlying meta-analyses, such as "class size," "teacher-student relationships," "direct instruction," and "feedback," and then determining their effect size, which can be calculated via comparing the averages of two conditions (e.g. a new vs. older curriculum, reducing class size from 25–30 to 15–20) or by comparing students over time after some intervention. The beauty of effect sizes is that, once computed, they can be reasonably compared across many interventions. There are many excellent sources for understanding effect sizes (Coe, 2012; Lipsey & Wilson, 2001). Like every other method, meta-analyses – and especially the innovative attempt in Visible Learning to construct a synthesis of meta-analyses – are, of course, not without their flaws, and it is, therefore, important to refer to some of these criticisms (cf. Snook et al., 2009; Zierer, 2016b).

The various influences generated from the multiple meta-analyses can be assigned to various domains: learners, family, school, teacher, curriculum, and teaching. The table below provides a summary of the procedure as a whole.[1]

This summary already reveals an important finding: There are domains that have been the topic of much research, such as teaching, and domains that have been the topic of fewer research syntheses, such as family. As important, there can be great variation in the dispersion of effect sizes within the domains: Whereas most of the factors in the domain of school, for instance, are clustered around an effect size of 0.2, the factors in the domain of teacher achieve effect sizes between 0.12 ("teacher education") and 0.90 ("teacher credibility"). Understanding this variance is important to building the case for the importance of teacher mind frames as one of the critical underlying factors underlying these many influences.

Across the 800 meta-analyses included in the meta-study, the variability of the effects can be shown in the following distribution (see Figure 0.4).

	FACTORS	META-ANALYSES	STUDIES	OVERALL EFFECT SIZE
Learners	19	152	11,909	0.39
Family	7	40	2,347	0.31
School	32	115	4,688	0.23
Teacher	12	41	2,452	0.47
Curriculum	25	135	10,129	0.45
Teaching	55	412	28,642	0.43

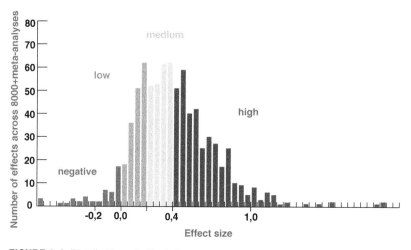

FIGURE 0.4 Distribution of effect size

Source: Hattie and Zierer (2017).

In many ways, this distribution shows that practically everything that happens in school and the classroom can lead to an increase in academic performance. To put it another way, 90 to 95 percent of what we do to learners increases their achievement. One might think that this would reassure us teachers, but that is not the case. The only thing this result illustrates is that people are learning all the time – sometimes despite us. This helps explain why almost everyone can claim "evidence" for their favorite influence. In many senses, you cannot prevent learning.

The key notion, however, is that we should be asking about the story underlying those influences greater than the average effect compared with those influences below the average effect (but still positive). This is the Visible Learning story and has been well rehearsed in other Visible Learning books and not recited here. The question this book addresses is related to the one big critical idea underlying success in making a difference to the learning lives of students – the mindframes of the educators.

How is this book organized?

Against this backdrop, we would like to introduce several general methodological considerations regarding the book itself. We have selected the following elements to illustrate the ten mindframes on the basis of findings from empirical educational research as outlined in the *Visible Learning* books.

- We know today that learning is more successful when teachers succeed in activating and taking account of the prior knowledge and previous experiences of their students. For this reason, each chapter begins with a questionnaire for self-reflection that was developed with the help of a survey of more than 500 teachers.

- We know that achievement gains in general and success in particular depend not only on knowledge and ability but also and especially on will and judgment of the teacher and students. For this reason, the questionnaires at the beginning of the chapters are designed to reveal the reader's own understandings, knowledge, will, and judgment.

- We know that clarity in regard to learning objectives is important for learning success. For this reason, we state the main messages of each chapter and present examples to illustrate it. This paves the way for an understanding of the procedure followed in the chapter.

- We know that an orientation toward problems, experience, and actions is an important element of successful instruction (cf. Merrill, 2002). For this reason, we provide recommendations for action and include sample problems and tasks for reflection as often as possible to illustrate the theoretical and empirical findings presented in the text.

- We know that summaries at the end of a lesson are conducive to learning. For this reason, we present a checklist at the end of each chapter to help readers review and practice the material.

- We know that learning involves deliberate practice. For this reason, we present exercises at the end of each chapter. These exercises refer to the questionnaire at the beginning of the chapter in order to assist making the learning visible. They focus on classroom practice and provide support in planning and analyzing lessons. Special emphasis is always placed on possibilities for cooperation and the search for evidence for one's own thought and actions.

- We know that expertise requires both competence and an appropriate mindframe. For this reason, we endeavor to address these two aspects repeatedly in this book and bring them into the conversation – for instance by encouraging considerations on mindframes with the help of the questionnaires at the beginning and the end of the chapters and by presenting evidence-based knowledge in the chapters themselves.

■ We hope that readers will want to follow up on these ideas and thus provide suggestions for further reading to review the material and study it in more depth.

Our hope in organizing the book in this fashion is that it becomes a workbook in a very real sense, a book that is at the same time demanding, challenging, and thought provoking; a book that helps readers to call their own mindframes into question, to develop their own skills, and so to foster their own educational expertise.

For whom is this book intended?

When one writes a book, one always has a particular audience in mind. Whom did we have in mind? The audience at the talks we have had the pleasure of giving on Visible Learning has always been something of a mixed bag, ranging from students, trainee teachers, and in-service teachers to school principals and administrators at schools and ministries. Occasionally, we have parents, Ministers of Education, and reporters. We kept all these groups in mind in writing this book and hope to offer something for each of them:

■ For students, we hope this book will provide insight into the current state of educational research and give them a chance to understand their own learning.

■ For teacher education students, we hope this book will provide support in acclimatizing themselves to how they need to think and interpret the world of students and classrooms. As will be seen, this is far more important than having tips and tricks of classroom management, curriculum and assessment knowledge, and know-how to build relations – although these all help to implement the ways of thinking that are most important.

■ For teachers, we aim for this book to be a source of inspiration that asks many questions concerning how they think about their own teaching and the importance of collaborating with other teachers to enhance, refine, and critique one's thinking.

■ For principals, we hope this book will give direction as to how they can motivate their teachers and aid them to work together to know they can all change the learning lives of all students and help them feed these beliefs with evidence of their impact.

■ For administrators at schools and ministries, we hope this book will serve to make it clear what challenges teachers are faced with and what support they need to be successful. Although the place of education is doubtlessly the interaction between the learner and the teacher, a respectful attitude and a focus on supporting the implementation of the ten mindframes on the part of administrators at schools and ministries can also have an enormous impact.

Finally, we hope this book will be of interest to anyone engaged with questions of education – whether in the school context or elsewhere. After all, learning follows similar principles in other domains as well, principles that depend on the competence and mindframes of the teachers, students, leaders, and parents.

Words of thanks

This book would not have been written without the direct and indirect cooperation of many people. First, we would like to mention the many schools and educational institutions we have been invited to in the past years to give talks about Visible Learning and in many thousands of schools to assist in implementing the principles of Visible Learning – on all six continents (we would welcome being invited to Antarctica, please). We hope to have given the educators at these institutions a worthwhile perspective on how they think and work. What we know for certain, however, is that we have picked up many useful ideas from every school and from the discussions with the teachers we met there. Many of them have found their way into this book.

John: When I wrote *Visible Learning*, the big challenge for me was to see the story hidden behind the multitude of data. While the task of collecting this data might have been quite time-consuming, it was easier collecting the data than interpreting it. Understanding the numerous findings takes even more time and involves constantly moving forward and backward again to ultimately bring all the aspects together. In doing so, I came to realize again and again that the main message of all the meta-analyses is the question of how teachers think, how they explain what they do. And depending on which mindframes guide this thinking, the teachers' influence on the children's learning differs. This idea may already be found in the work of David Berliner, John Dewey, Paulo Freire, and many others. In the end, I attempted to describe various shapes and forms of those mindframes that are crucial for a teacher's success. After several attempts, and after receiving constructive criticism from researchers and practitioners, we have now described ten of them. I would thus like to use this occasion to thank everyone who has pointed out difficulties in my formulation of the mindframes, who has discussed, debated, and also argued with me. Without these discussions, it would not have been possible to achieve the degree of descriptive incisiveness I see in this book. The task for me was then to subject the mindframes defined in this way to an empirical examination. In this context, I would like to give my special thanks to Debra Masters and Heidi Lesson. Above all, I would like to use this occasion to thank the numerous translators of Visible Learning for the many critical questions they asked: the colleagues at Cognition in New Zealand; at Corwin in the USA, Canada, and Australia; at Challenging Learning in Norway, Sweden, and Denmark; and at OSIRIS in Great Britain. Moreover, I would like to thank my colleagues at the Melbourne Graduate School of Education. They are the ones who put Visible Learning into practice day in and day out, thus making many important discoveries and generating new ideas. However, my greatest thanks goes to Klaus for his ideas, his inspiration, his tenacity, his sincerity, and his loyalty as a true friend. It was a pleasure to write this book with him, bridging the distance between Australia and Germany as well as language differences to bring together stimulating and challenging perspectives. Writing a book clearly takes a lot of time, support, and perseverance – and I would, therefore, like to thank my family, especially Janet, my life partner, biggest critic and supporter, co-worker and provider of much feedback, and our now-adult children: Joel, Kat, Kyle, Jess, Kieran, Aleisha, Edna, and Patterson. I would like to dedicate this book to all of my grandchildren – may there be many of them – and thus especially to Emma, my first granddaughter.

Klaus: I would first like to mention the educational policy-maker Georg Eisenreich, Bavarian State Secretary, and Mathias Brodkorb, former Minister of Education in Mecklenburg-Vorpommern, with whom I have had many in-depth discussions about school and teaching. I would also like to thank Johannes Bastian, whose suggestion that I do a series on the Hattie study for the journal *Pädagogik* was instrumental in motivating me to realize my long-harbored plan of writing *Kenne deinen Einfluss!: Visible Learning für die Unterrichtspraxis* with John. *Pädagogik* has since published a four-part series that takes up individual elements of this book. I would like to thank Wolfgang Beywl for our cooperation over the years, which began with the translation of John's studies into German and has since continued in various contexts. This cooperation has always been marked by reliability and loyalty. And, finally, I would like to thank Joachim Kahlert, who managed the change in roles from my university teacher to my boss to my colleague with flying colors and who has now been an important dialogue partner for years. Special thanks go to my brother Rudi Zierer, who has been my most constant companion and my most critical reader over the years. We discussed and scrutinized many issues mentioned in this book on numerous rounds of jogging. I owe my greatest thanks to John for his willingness to embark on this path with me, which was never going to be an easy one from the beginning even just on account of the great physical distance that separates us. Nevertheless, we succeeded in making sure that this challenge was always also a pleasure – above all, because our cooperation was always marked by mutual trust, transparency, and constructive criticism. And last, but not least, I would like to thank my family: my three children Viktoria, Zacharias, and Quirin, who constantly challenge me in my role as a father and show me what seems sensible from a theoretical and empirical perspective but is of no use in practice and also, vice versa, what goes wrong in practice and can be explained from a theoretical and empirical perspective, and my wife, Maria, who (usually) enjoys reflecting on our attempts at child rearing late at night.

John Hattie & Klaus Zierer
Melbourne and Marklkofen, July 2017

Note

1 We always cite the most current statistics available in this book. At the time of printing, these were the updated statistics included in *Visible Learning for Teachers*.

I am an evaluator of my impact on student learning

QUESTIONNAIRE FOR SELF-REFLECTION

Assess yourself by rating your agreement with the following statements: 1 = strongly disagree, 5 = strongly agree.

I am very good at . . .

making my impact on student learning visible.

using methods for making my impact on student learning visible.

I know perfectly well . . .

that student achievements make my impact visible.

that student achievements help me to maximize my impact.

My goal is always to . . .

evaluate my impact on student learning.

use multiple methods of measuring student achievement to assess my impact on student learning.

I am thoroughly convinced . . .

that I need to evaluate my impact on student learning regularly and systematically.

that I need to use student learning to asses my impact.

VIGNETTE

Please imagine two teachers. Both prepare their lessons properly and conscientiously. While the one teacher formulates his or her central message as "I want to teach a good lesson," the maxim of the other teacher is "I would like to make my impact on the learners visible at the end of the lesson." Both mindframes are convincing at first glance. At second glance, however, the difference becomes clear: The first teacher will be satisfied if she or he feels at the end of the lesson that the lesson has gone well, the learners have participated well, no disturbances have interrupted the flow of the lesson, and the most important content was explained. All of this is, of course, important for the other teacher as well. But she or he will not rely on feeling and will look for evidence. As a result, at least at the end of the lesson, but probably during the lesson as well, the first teacher will have to slip into the role of the evaluator again and again, listening instead of talking, making learning visible and showing the students what they can do now – and what they cannot. The lesson will not end without this teacher trying to make his or her influence visible by means of the students' learning performance.

What is this chapter about?

This vignette tries to pinpoint the core message of this mindframe: Educational expertise is shown by how teachers think about what they do. One of the most crucial questions is whether teachers want to know about their impact and make it visible. Teachers who have set themselves this goal and are consistently trying to implement it are fundamentally different from teachers who do not ask themselves this question. "Visible Learning" and "Know thy impact" become the core message of this mindframe – and the core message of this book.

After reading this chapter, you should be able to explain, in light of this core message:

- the progress from proficiency to enhanced achievement.
- the evidence of the factors "providing formative evaluation" and "response to intervention."
- what is meant by the notion "Teachers are to DIE for."
- how individual feedback works.

Which factors from Visible Learning support this mindframe?

When you walk into a classroom and say to yourself, "My job here is to evaluate my impact," then students are the major beneficiaries. This is by far the most important of all mindframes and dominates as the major message from the Visible Learning research. Of course, this begs the moral purpose question of what we mean by impact. It also means we have to continually adjust and refine what we are doing to maximize the impact for each student, and it means we often need to stop talking and listen for our impact.

There are many forms of impact, such as a sense of belonging as a learner, the will and thrill of learning, respect for self and respect for others, higher achievement and attitudes, positive disposition, and social sensitivity. There are many ways to make this impact visible: artifacts of student work, observation of students' learning, tests and assignments, listening to interactions among students, and privileging student voice about their learning.

We must ensure each student progresses in his or her achievement journey across the usual school disciplines. While, of course, the topics of these disciplines can be quite different depending on country or even jurisdiction, some form of academic achievement is present in every classroom. It is not the task of this book to debate this curriculum but to be reminded of Michael Young's (2013) claim that we often send students to school to be exposed to what they would not be exposed to if they did not go. Also, to note that most curricula are based on "adult group think": groups of adults deciding on scope and sequence of topics. Rarely is curriculum based on how students actually progress (because there is so little research on that topic). Indeed, if we lined up various curricula from different jurisdictions, it is for certain that they would differ in this scope and sequence and the choice of curricula topics – but each would be presented as the one and proper solution.

Whatever the content, the progress is the critical task we ask of teachers and students. Developing an understanding of progression can either be explicit and provided to teachers or it can be intuitive and worked through by teachers in the moment within the classroom. Given the many students in a class, the latter is more frequent, simply because learning is rarely linear and follows someone's dictates of how learning progresses – it is more staccato, and it is likely that progression can differ depending on where each student starts.

3

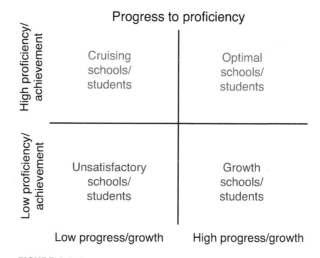

FIGURE 1.1 Progress to proficiency

Note the emphasis on progression to achievement. Too often, high achievement is privileged and although, of course, we all want high achievement, an overemphasis on achievement can lead to distortions in understanding the impact of educators. The relation between progress and achievement can be expressed in many ways, such as in Figure 1.1. On the x-axis, we have placed achievement, and on the y-axis, growth or progress. We can apply tentative labels to each of the four quadrants. Success is thus not always high achievement (who wants to be a cruising school or student) but is defined as high progress. No matter where the student starts, he or she deserves at least a year's growth for a year's input. And knowing that this is the focus of impact is the fundamental starting point of understanding impact.

To understand what a "year's growth" means, we have to consult multiple sources. It can include looking at effect sizes over time, examples of student work over a year, indexing to a year's curriculum claims – but critically understanding this growth involves conferring with other teachers. This is related to the mindframe "I collaborate with my peers and my students about my conceptions of progress and my impact."

Providing formative evaluation

In Figure 1.2, the factor "providing formative evaluation" arouses interest, as it is among the most powerful factors in Visible Learning, with an effect size of 0.90.

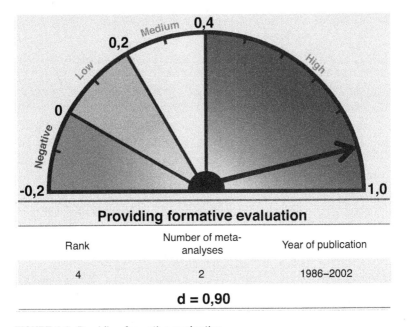

Providing formative evaluation

Rank	Number of meta-analyses	Year of publication
4	2	1986–2002

d = 0,90

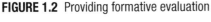

FIGURE 1.2 Providing formative evaluation

Source: Hattie and Zierer (2017).

What does formative evaluation involve, and what makes it so effective? Michael Scriven (1967) distinguishes between formative and summative evaluation of instructional processes. Whereas formative evaluation is conducted during an intervention, allowing the teacher to use the resulting data to improve the instructional process, summative evaluation is conducted at the end of the intervention and is thus an evaluation of its result. (Note that this means that there is no such notion as formative or summative assessment, as any assessment can be used to make formative evaluation [during the lesson] or summative evaluation [at the end of the lesson].) The effects on student learning will obviously be different in each case: Results from a formative evaluation can still be used to benefit the learners, whereas results from a summative evaluation serve only as feedback for the teacher – although it can be used later by learners in the next set of lessons. These characteristics show why formative evaluation is often seen as being closely related to feedback, and indeed there are many aspects in which they overlap. However, there are two important, if not to say crucial, distinctions between these factors. First, while feedback can take the form of teacher-to-student feedback or student-to-teacher feedback, formative evaluation provides feedback from the learner to the teacher: It helps the teacher modify instruction, see the effects of their teaching so far, and hints as to where to go next in their teaching. Second, while feedback focuses on all aspects of teaching, formative evaluation focuses on the goals of the learning process and seeks to determine whether the learners have reached these goals – yet. The secret to the success of a formative evaluation lies in these two distinctions. After all, it is focusing on whether learners have reached the goals or success criteria of the lessons – and it is the teacher who needs to have the competence and mindframe to seek this information and draw the right conclusions from it for the further course of the learning process. Of course, students can also use formative evaluation to tweak, change, and modify their own learning, but it is formative evaluation about and to the teacher that has the greatest impact.

Response to intervention

The term "response to intervention," "RTI" for short, originated in the United States, and refers to an approach designed especially for children and youths with learning difficulties (see Figure 1.3). It thus has its roots in special education but has since been applied to general education within the context of inclusion – with as much success. The secret to the success of the "response to intervention" factor lies in the teacher's continuous adjustment of the lesson (intervention) and the resulting benefit derived from the learners (response). It enables the teacher to continually adjust the instruction to match the current learning level of the students.

This process is organized in a so-called multilevel prevention model generally made up of three tiers: At the first tier, the teacher holds a regular lesson for all learners that meets current quality criteria. At the second tier, the teacher intervenes on behalf of the learners who were incapable of achieving the desired learning success in the first step. This support involves applying appropriate methods for measuring learning levels and is given in small groups for a set period of time. At the third tier, the teacher provides supplementary instruction for learners who did not achieve the desired learning success during the intervention on the second tier.

At this third tier, interventions generally take the form of one-on-one instruction, allowing the teacher to provide more individualized and intense support to the students who need it. Hence, the three tiers differ in regard to group size, degree of individualization, and duration. It

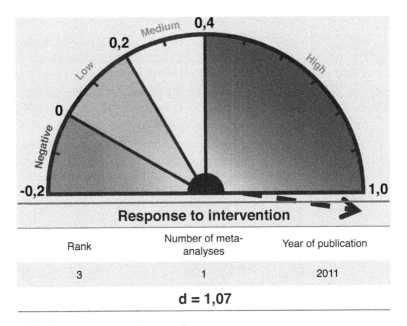

FIGURE 1.3 Response to intervention

Source: Hattie and Zierer (2017).

is important to remark that the teacher needs to demand continuous feedback on learning success between all the tiers and during all the interventions in order to provide the learners the best possible support.

Teachers are to DIE for

This is akin to the notions within RTI, with the emphasis on excellent diagnosis, appropriate interventions, and excellent evaluation of the interventions. Too often, there is an overemphasis on the teaching or interventions, even when adoption of these interventions is not related to what students already know or do not know, and too often, the same intervention or teaching method is reproduced and students are blamed for not attending, not being motivated, or not being smart. Instead, if students do not learn the first time, a change in the method of teaching is more likely to move these students forward.

These three aspects certainly highlight the expertise needed by teachers, and there is a continuing interplay between them. Such a philosophy demands higher level cognitive decision skills by teachers; demands the willingness to say "I was wrong in my choice of method of intervention" and need to change what I do or to say "I was right in my choice of interventions," as they led to me successfully teaching these students; and demands teachers engaging in collaborative inquiry about their diagnoses, interventions, and evaluations. Rushing to interventions, trying some new method, or adopting a new teaching approach without attending to the needs of the students is common and can be destructive. If the new approach does not work, it is often the case that teachers say the students were not receptive, were from the wrong postcode, or did not commit to the work. Beware of educators with solutions – if these solutions do not remediate the needs of the students.

- Diagnosis – that is, understanding what each student brings to the lesson, his or her motivations, and willingness to engage.
- Intervention – that is, having multiple interventions such that if one does not work with the student, the teacher changes to another intervention. It also involves knowing the high probability interventions, knowing when to switch, and certainly not creating blame language about why the student is not learning.
- Evaluation – that is, knowing the skills, having multiple methods, and collaboratively debating the magnitude of impact from the interventions.

These three parts of maximizing impact may need a fourth – quality implementation. A great intervention poorly implemented is more a reflection of the implementation than the intervention. This is why we need care when we see that certain teaching interventions have high effect sizes – these are probability statements about the likelihood of an intervention. Care is still needed to ensure fidelity of implementation. So perhaps it should be Teachers are to DIIE for!

Where can I start?

These considerations lead us to an idea advanced in *Visible Learning for Teachers* (Hattie, 2014): It is possible with the help of regular tests to calculate an individual effect size for each learner. This involves taking the formulas described in the preface of this book and entering the test results into a table. After calculating the mean values, the standard deviations, and the mean value of the standard deviations, one can create the following table with individual effect sizes.

STUDENT	TIME	TIME 2	GROWTH ES
Julia	44	48	0.28
Julio	57	66	0.62
Kate	37	52	1.03
Megan	82	78	−0.28
Jennifer	39	62	1.58
Matt	46	64	1.24
Yun	57	73	1.10
Pablo	63	60	−0.21
Robert	68	71	0.21
Max	29	35	0.41
Rodriguez	67	68	0.07
Average	53.55	61.55	
SD		14.54	
Effect size		0.55	

FIGURE 1.4 Effect size

To calculate effect sizes for individual students, we assume that each student contributes similarly to the overall variance (and given we are making an assumption, we need extra care in interpretation; check any surprises with alternative evidence) and then use the pooled spread (standard deviation) as an estimator for each student. We use the following formula:

$$\text{Effect size} = \frac{\text{Mean}_{\text{end of treatment}} - \text{Mean}_{\text{beginning of treatment}}}{\text{Standard Deviation}}$$

In the previous case, there are now some important questions for teachers. Why did Jennifer and Matt achieve such high gains, and why did Megan, Robert, and Julia achieve such low gains? The data, obviously, do not ascribe the reasons, but they do provide the best evidence to lead to these important causal explanations. (Note that, in this case, it is not necessarily a fact that it was the struggling students who made the lowest and the brightest who made the highest gains.)

Given that there is an assumption (that each student contributes to the spread similarly), the most important issue is the questions that these data create: What possible explanations could there be for those students who achieved higher impacts and for those who achieved lower impacts? This then allows evidence to be used to formulate the right questions. Only teachers can look for the reasons, and as always, we need to look for triangulation about these reasons and devise strategies for these students.

There are some things of which you should be aware when using effect sizes:

A. Caution should be used with small sample sizes: The smaller the sample, the more care should be taken to cross-validate the findings. Any sample size of fewer than 30 students can be considered "small" and thus care is nearly always needed.

B. It is crucial to look for outlier students. In a small sample, a few outliers can skew the effect sizes, and they may need special consideration (with questions including Why did they grow so much more than the other students? or Why did they not grow as much as the other students?); the effect sizes may even need to be recalculated with these students omitted. If the overall effect does not change much when outliers are included compared with excluded, then it is probably reasonable to leave them in. If quite different, they must be omitted from the calculations.

The advantage of using the effect-size method is that effect sizes can be interpreted across tests, classes, times, and so forth. Although it makes much sense to use the same test for the pre- and post-test, this is not always necessary. For example, in some longitudinal tests, the tests are different each time, but they have been built to measure the same dimension both times and calibrated to take into account different difficulties of the items in the tests. There are some forms of scores that are less amenable to interpreting; for example, percentiles, stanines, and NCE scores have sufficiently unusual properties that effect sizes as calculated earlier can yield misleading results.

Using effect sizes invites teachers to think about using assessment to help to estimate progress and to reframe instruction to better tailor learning for individuals or groups of students. It asks teachers to consider reasons why some students have progressed and others have not – as a consequence of their teaching. This is an example of "evidence into action."

CHECKLIST

- Make your impact on student learning visible at the end of the lesson.
- Use this information to plan the next lesson.
- Implement in the intervention phase procedures to measure your impact on student achievement and to make learning visible in order to be able to deal with this in the intervention phase.
- Use formative evaluation to make learning visible.

EXERCISES

- Return to the self-reflection questionnaire at the beginning of the chapter and fill it in with a different color. Where has your view of things changed and, above all, why? Discuss your assessments with a colleague.
- Plan your next lesson including a phase in which students have to show what they have learned. Discuss your experiences with your colleagues.
- Design with your colleagues two tests for individual feedback and provide this formative assessment in class. Discuss your experiences with your colleagues and develop this tool on an evidence-based basis.

I see assessment as informing my impact and next steps

QUESTIONNAIRE FOR SELF-REFLECTION

Assess yourself by rating your agreement with the following statements: 1 = strongly disagree, 5 = strongly agree.

I am very good at . . .

adapting my teaching when my students do not achieve their learning goals.

using the achievements of my students to draw conclusions on my thoughts concerning goals, content, methods, and media.

I know perfectly well . . .

that student achievements are feedback on the success of my teaching.

that student achievements allow me to draw conclusions on my thoughts concerning goals, content, methods, and media.

My goal is always to . . .

measure the achievement levels of my students regularly and systematically.

use objective methods of measuring student achievement to assess the success of my teaching.

I am thoroughly convinced . . .

that I need to check the achievement levels of my students regularly and systematically.

that I need to use objective methods of measuring student achievement to assess the success of my teaching.

VIGNETTE

It is a situation every experienced teacher knows: You put a lot of time and effort into grading an assignment. Exhausted but satisfied at a job well done, you put the finishing touches on the corrections and begin thinking about how you will discuss the mistakes with the students individually and answer any remaining questions they may have. But what happens when you return the assignments? Most of the students stuff them in their schoolbags without even casting a glance at the comments you made on them. At first, you ask yourself the perfectly reasonable question: Why do I go through all the trouble to grade these assignments when the learners cannot even be bothered to take a look at how they did? Upon closer consideration, however, you come to realize that teachers do not just grade assignments for the learners. Perhaps even more important, they do it for themselves.

What is this chapter about?

This vignette illustrates this chapter's main message: Student assessments are not important feedback just for learners. They are even more useful for teachers themselves, because they provide indications about the lesson they gave – and accordingly also about all relevant pedagogical issues, such as whether the students achieved the learning goals, understood the content, and found the methods appropriate and the media helpful. In this chapter, we refer to "assessments" as any task that the teacher or students uses to evaluate questions such as How are they going? Where are they going? and helps address Where to next? Thus, it could be a test, comments on a performance, discussion or presentation, or an assigned task. The mindframe is about any evaluation of judgment that is made – and the typical claim is that these evaluations serve to help students improve, and yes they can. But the mindframe that is desired is for teachers to consider assessments as powerful feedback to them about their impact – and thence the students will be the ultimate beneficiaries.

When you finish reading this chapter, you should be able to take this message as a basis for explaining:

■ how significant the factors "time on task," "providing formative evaluation," and "response to intervention" are.

- why assignments, tests, quizzes, and so forth are among the most important means of making student learning as well as the teacher's influence visible.

- how a sensible use of interpreting artifacts of student work can contribute to the cultivation of this mindframe.

Which factors from Visible Learning support this mindframe?

Apart from the school system, class size, and homework assignments, there is hardly an issue in the school context that sparks such heated debates as the point or pointlessness of grades. This contentious issue, however, is often not the grades themselves but the way we deal with them: Do we understand grades as an unalterable stigmatization or as a more intense form of feedback? Do they block learning pathways because they demotivate students, or do they foster motivation because they encourage students to try harder? Do they signal to the student that the work is now over? An idea frequently advanced as an alternative is to replace grades with other forms of assessment. Two such suggestions that have always been popular and have inspired much hope is verbal assessment, or written comments. Proponents claim that it would revolutionize educational assessment, improve learning for everyone, and lead to more social justice.

Indeed, it is possible to find situations in which both grades and other forms of educational assessment are misused: grades as a means of repression and verbal assessments as blanket statements with no individual relevance, to name just two negative examples.

The most powerful way to redress these negative examples is this mindframe. If teachers consider assessments as primarily feedback to them, then this can alter the nature of the assessments, can provide more information about how to adjust the teaching, and help understand where best to move next – for the teacher and particularly then for the student.

Three factors in Visible Learning that demonstrate what makes up a professional mindframe in this context are "time on task," and the already mentioned "providing formative evaluation," and "response to intervention."

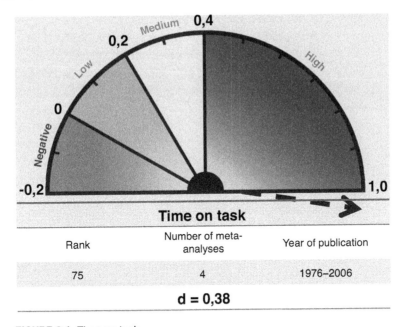

Time on task

Rank	Number of meta-analyses	Year of publication
75	4	1976–2006

d = 0,38

FIGURE 2.1 Time on task

Source: Hattie and Zierer (2017).

Time on task

The factor "time on task" is hardly ever missing from lists of criteria for good instruction (see Figure 2.1). Accordingly, the effect size of 0.38 it achieves in Visible Learning is respectable, even though it does not quite reach the bar of 0.4. However, this solid result is no protection against the myths that hamper the understanding of this factor: Time on task is often regarded as a simple matter of keeping the learners busy with as few interruptions as possible. This leads to lessons in which the teacher moves seamlessly from one method to the next, leaving the impression of a smooth learning experience for the learners. The mere fact that all the learners were engaged during such a lesson is then seen as an indication that the lesson was successful. This understanding of student achievement is not optimal and can obstruct the path to the mindframe "I see assessment as informing my impact and next steps." Understood in the right way, time on task does not just mean that the learners are busy all the time but that they spend the majority of the learning time working on the tasks they have been assigned, feel challenged by them to an appropriate degree, and test their limits in working on them. Thus, there is a sense of "deliberate" use of the time available, and not just time on task to practice, practice, and practice (particularly if the practice is overlearning of the wrong, incomplete, or irrelevant). This is also the main message of the meta-analyses: Extending learning time alone (as a purely structural measure) has little effect on learning. What is crucial is rather to challenge the learners, to confront them with tasks that they are just barely capable of completing, and to have learners work on these tasks in a team. This investment in learning is a core skill needed to be taught to students, as some do not know how to use time wisely.

Our account of the factors "time on task," "providing formative evaluation," and "response to intervention" shows that the key to successful teaching and learning processes lies in measuring student achievements and applying the results in the further course of a lesson – especially by the teacher. These teachers can make learning visible and draw the right conclusions for their teaching, and then the greater their students' learning progress can be. The task of making learning visible doubtlessly constitutes a challenge for teachers in two respects: On the one hand, it requires the competence to be familiar with appropriate multiple methods and apply them adequately, but on the other hand, it also requires a belief in these methods and the motivation to implement them. Both together form the basis for the mindframe "Regard student assessments as feedback for you about you."

Assignments, tests, quizzes, and so forth – more than just a tedious obligation?

Pedagogical literature reminds us again and again that scholastic achievement cannot be reduced to the physical formula "achievement = work + time." Pedagogical achievement is not just product-oriented but also process-oriented and invokes aspects of personality. There needs to be a willingness to achieve, a willingness to invest in learning, and an openness to new experiences (which may question what we already know). An important instructional instrument for this purpose is assignments – understood here and in the following as a synonym for all kinds of graded schoolwork, tests, and other means of measuring achievement at school.

Of course, assignments do not have the sole purpose of determining grades for the report card; they are the foundation for diagnosing student achievements and analyzing instruction: On the one hand, they enable the teacher to gauge learning conditions, methods, and levels and to obtain information on how the students learn and work. On the other hand, they provide the teacher information on the achievement and suitability of the learning goals, the content, the methods, and the media, enabling corresponding conclusions. They can serve to introduce a lesson, accompany a lesson, or conclude a lesson. Because assignments are part of the lesson, they also are subject to its conditions, consisting of the relation between the teacher, the learners, and the material, as well as the situational and individual conditions, and all of these conditions can influence the outcome of assignments.

Although the design and evaluation of assignments are connected, common practice makes the extent of the problems clear: Apart from any comments the teacher writes at the end of a graded assignment, the only data and information to be collected and evaluated are the grades entered into a student list, the grading scale, and the calculation of the grade point average. Obviously, this will not lead to a meaningful diagnosis of the learning process or an effective analysis of the lesson: It does not fulfill any of the criteria of educational achievement. On the contrary, it regards achievement as the product of a single cumulative grade. It disregards the process, takes no account of the individual aspects of student achievement, and thus ignores all the surrounding factors of instruction. To illustrate this by means of an example, consider the fact that a grade of F represents the same achievement whether it is given to a high-achieving learner who did not reach his or her usual level of achievement due to illness or to a low-achieving learner who perhaps even worked well for his or her standards. The final grade alone need not be taken as the basis for a diagnosis of instruction, let alone an analysis.

But what to do when the results are too "good" or "poor"? The former case should actually not present any difficulties: Is it not the goal of all pedagogical efforts for all children to achieve the learning goal? This problem crops up repeatedly, however, particularly in comparisons between individual classes or schools. In our view, the common practice of grading on a curve to correct for results that are too good and achieve a normal distribution or an "acceptable" grade point average of 2.0, C grade, or some minimally accepted score is inadmissible – particularly as it is not pedagogically justifiable to penalize children who are making high levels of progress for being in a class with a lot of high-achieving children. The teacher is responsible for considering whether the assignment was too easy (or too hard) this time and for drawing any necessary conclusions for his or her instruction and future assessment. Results that are too poor present teachers with a similar problem: Should the children be penalized if their teacher perhaps did not succeed in designing the instruction in accordance with the criteria being tested? Grading on a curve seems acceptable in this case, because the teacher needs to take the side of the children. It is the job of the teacher to use his or her knowledge about the class situation to decide where the limit lies in concrete cases. The average amount of points for each task can be of help, as can work in teams for specific grade levels. However, the two extremes discussed here illustrate how closely linked the preceding and subsequent instruction is with the construction and evaluation of assignments.

The worksheet is dead, long live the worksheet – a criticism of overloaded worksheets

That teachers generally have loads and loads of worksheets is not just the fault of the internet. It is also a result of the strong tendency many of them have of collecting everything that has anything to do with their own instruction. They fill their shelves with binder after binder and soon feel confident in having a worksheet to whip out in every instructional situation. The more attractively arranged, the more creative, the more fun the worksheet is, the more likely it will be used. Yet caution is advised.

Worksheets that resemble artwork are certainly nice to look at, but they often have a critical shortcoming when it comes to learning. As demonstrated by the cognitive load theory, discussed in Chapter 10 "I focus on learning and the language of learning," they tend to divert attention away from the task at hand and to the artwork themselves, which are essentially nothing but decoration and serve merely to liven up (or even distract from) the lesson. There is the obvious danger that this decoration can lead to an overload of working memory, leaving the learners with only little resources or even none at all to then actually complete the learning tasks. To make matters worse, the motivation this decoration provides is largely extrinsic, which is again connected with the initial learning levels of the students and should, therefore, be applied only sparingly. This problem may be illustrated by the multitude of pedagogical creations designed for mathematics instruction: arithmetic towers, arithmetic wheels, arithmetic fields, arithmetic pyramids, and so on. These methods are certainly interesting in general, because they are full of pedagogical creativity and can liven up a lesson. However, if they hardly include any tasks because most of the space is taken up by the artwork, and if the few tasks they do include are difficult for the learners to understand because the artwork is in the way, then they lose their pedagogical value: The small number of tasks simply provides too little reinforcement and practice and requires too much cognitive effort to understand.

A principle that can be helpful in this context is that of Ockham's razor. The scholastic philosopher William of Ockham argued that if one is presented with a wide variety of hypotheses for explaining reality, the one to pick is that involving the least variables and assumptions – incidentally an idea already advanced by Aristotle. Transferred to a pedagogical context, this means that if one has a wide variety of methods on hand for testing whether the students have achieved the learning goal, the ones to pick are those that can make learning visible with the least possible additional effort – and all other pedagogical gimmicks should be left out. In mathematics instruction, to return to the example presented earlier, a sensible course might, therefore, be to write the type of task on a piece of paper without the artwork as often as necessary and have the learners make the necessary calculations.

Ockham's razor is backed by epistemological theory and has been empirically validated in a number of fields. It is, therefore, worth it from a pedagogical standpoint to consider following the principle of parsimony rather than the principle of variety.

Where can I start?

In the following, we present three examples of methods for making learning visible at the end of the lesson as suggestions to help you come up with your own ideas, which you can then develop, try out, and discuss with your colleagues.

The first example is a mathematics lesson on the formulas for the sine and cosine – embedded in an instructional sequence called "What is the meaning of longitude and latitude?" (see Figure 2.2). The teacher writes the following synthesis on the chalkboard:

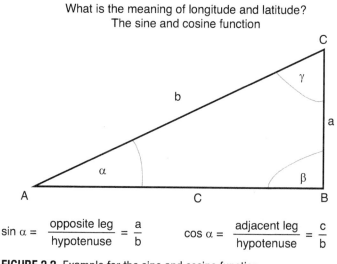

sin α = $\dfrac{\text{opposite leg}}{\text{hypotenuse}} = \dfrac{a}{b}$ cos α = $\dfrac{\text{adjacent leg}}{\text{hypotenuse}} = \dfrac{c}{b}$

FIGURE 2.2 Example for the sine and cosine function

Source: Hattie and Zierer (2017).

The learners copy this drawing into their notebooks. This serves to activate the material and is at the same time an initial and important means of reinforcing and reviewing it – think back on the forgetting curve described in the context of the mindframe "See learning as hard work" and have the learners write things in their notebooks and take responsibility for their learning as often as possible. The teacher follows this up with further exercises on the formulas before asking the learners to close their notebooks at the end of the lesson and confronting them with the task of completing the following drawing (see Figure 2.3).

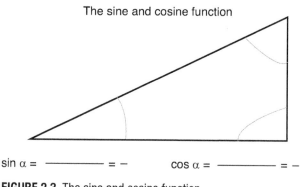

sin α = ———— = —   cos α = ———— = —

FIGURE 2.3 The sine and cosine function

Source: Hattie and Zierer (2017).

This task is located at the unistructural level – an appropriate level of challenge for an introductory lesson, particularly when one considers that a deep understanding (relational level and extended abstract) builds on a solid surface understanding (unistructural and multistructural level) (cf. a detailed explanation of these levels can be found in Chapter 5).

The second example is a quiz on the most important terms of the lesson. Because a quiz is a different form of achievement than the initial learning during the lesson, this task can already be classified as belonging to the multistructural level. At the end of a lesson in which various deciduous trees were introduced on the basis of their leaves and fruits, the worksheet for making the learning outcome visible – solution: "all right" – might look like this:

		1)	A	C	O	R	N		
	2)		A	L	D	E	R		
		3)	L	I	M	E			
	4)		B	I	R	C	H		
		5)	W	I	L	L	O	W	
		6)	M	A	G	N	O	L	I	A
7)		B	E	E	C	H			
		8)	N	U	T				

Depending on the achievement level of the learners, the numbers 1) to 8) could also be replaced by pictures of leaves and fruits, complemented by texts, or extended by an appropriate description read out loud by the teacher.

The third example involves formulating an open question, encouraging the learners to develop a deep understanding of the material learned. The task is assigned at the end of a lesson on Picasso and his artworks (cf. Hattie, 2014, p. 61):

What did Picasso aim to express in his painting Guernica? *Explain your answer.*

These three examples attempt to demonstrate that it is not all that difficult to develop ideas for your own thinking and teaching activity.

It is essentially a matter of asking yourself how the teaching process influences the learning process and searching for evidence to make the connection between these two processes visible. The most important thing is to succeed in not just collecting the data but also reflecting on and interpreting the data with your next lesson in mind.

Developing and implementing methods like these, as well as all forms of assignments, tests, and quizzes, is one of the most important tasks of teachers around the world.

CHECKLIST

Reflect on the following points next time you plan a lesson:

- See student achievements as what they are: feedback about you and for you.
- Consider the learning process in close connection with the teaching process.
- Interpret the mistakes your learners make with your teaching in mind.
- Include a phase at the end of the lesson in which you make learning visible.
- Integrate methods for this purpose into your lesson plan, taking into account both the current learning levels of the students and the level of challenge of the tasks you plan to assign.
- Reflect on the data you collected in regard to your pedagogical thinking and activity in general and your instruction in particular.
- Take notes on what you want to include later on in an assignment while you are planning the instructional sequence.
- Decide early on what tasks at the unistructural, multistructural, relational and extended abstract levels you should include in an assignment.
- Discuss the level of challenge you defined for the lesson with a colleague. Consider student achievements and check whether the level was appropriate.
- Use assignments to clarify the following questions: Which of my goals did I achieve in the lesson? What material did I successfully get across to the learners? Which methods turned out to be useful for fostering learning? Which media were useful for fostering learning?

- Double-check to make sure your students have learned the material, even if you believe they have: Knowing it is better than believing it in this case.

EXERCISES

- Go back to the questionnaire for self-reflection at the start of the chapter and complete it again in a different color. Where and, more important, why has your perspective on the statements changed? Discuss your self-assessment with a colleague.
- Design a method for checking whether the students have achieved the learning goals at the end of a lesson. Implement it and reflect on the results, first on your own and then with a colleague.
- Consider the unistructural, multistructural, relational and extended abstract levels in constructing and evaluating your next assignment. Get together with a colleague and attempt together to implement the possibilities described in this chapter for evaluating assignments.

I collaborate with my peers and my students about my conceptions of progress and my impact

---

QUESTIONNAIRE FOR SELF-REFLECTION

Assess yourself by rating your agreement with the following statements: 1 = strongly disagree, 5 = strongly agree.

I am very good at . . .

saving time by sharing work with other teachers.

sharing responsibility in a team.

I know perfectly well . . .

that failures can be overcome in a team.

that responsibility can be shared in a team.

My goal is always to . . .

consolidate strengths through teamwork.

overcome failures in my team.

I am thoroughly convinced . . .

that strengths can be consolidated in a team.

that it is important to cooperate with my colleagues.

VIGNETTE

How does a lawyer deal with a case that seems hopeless? What options are open to a journalist whose inquiries lead to seemingly contradictory facts? What does a scientist do when she reaches a dead end with her research? What successful people do in such cases is enter into a dialogue and try to solve their problems by cooperating with others.

What is this chapter about?

This vignette illustrates this chapter's main message: Educational expertise is a product of exchange and cooperation. Lone wolves can be successful, but they can be even more successful if they work together with others. This is particularly important for developing a sense of community among individuals.

When you finish reading this chapter, you should be able to take this message as a basis for explaining:

- how significant the factors "micro-teaching," "professional development," and "school size" are.
- what is meant by collective intelligence and how individuals can benefit from it.
- what conditions need to be fulfilled for successful team teaching.

Which factors from Visible Learning support this mindframe?

There are without doubt many teachers who seek to exchange and cooperate with each other. It would thus be wrong to suggest that teachers do not work together with their colleagues at all. It is unfortunate, however, that this cooperation is not always put into actual practice everywhere and is largely neglected in teacher education programs, where it is not systematically required and fostered. More important, the focus of collaboration needs to be about the impact and effects on students. We need to share how we think and evaluate our impact much more than discuss curriculum, assessment tasks, and sharing engaging activities.

The importance and necessity of exchange and cooperation is often illustrated by means of biological comparisons: Ant and bee colonies are classic examples of how much benefit the individual can derive from the community and of how the whole can be greater than the sum of its part. Although these two analogies do not work at every level – considering neither the greater diversity among humans and the value of an open society – both describe an essential aspect of community in a democracy and, therefore, serve to illustrate a key message: Humans too can benefit from exchange and cooperation.

A number of factors in Visible Learning provide empirical evidence for this argumentation, in particular "teachers' collective efficacy," "micro-teaching," and "professional development."

Collective efficacy

There will be a new #1 in the list of influences from Visible Learning – teachers' collective efficacy. This comes from Eells's (2011) dissertation where she summarized 26 studies, leading to a very high d = 1.23 on student achievement. This effect was high across all school subjects and at all levels of schooling (elementary, middle, and high). The message is clear: How teachers collectively think about their impact and student progress is most relevant to the success for their students.

Teachers' collective efficacy refers to the enhanced confidence to overcome any barriers and limitations and have the collective belief that all students in this school can gain more than a year's growth for a year's input. Clearly, this screams for leadership in the school to develop an organization climate, create school norms about collaborating, and creating the time and direction to enable all teachers in the school to share in this sense of confidence and have high expectations to make the difference. We need to be very mindful, however, that this enhanced collective efficacy needs to be fed by evidence that it is having the desired impact on student learning. It is not all growth mindset but evidence-informed mindset that all can grow.

Eells's research is based on two major notions. First, the idea that we need to have confidence in our capability to organize and teach students to produce given outcomes – this relates to "I cause learning" in an earlier chapter. When we have appropriately high expectations about these outcomes, we are more likely to indeed get higher outcomes from our students. (For sure, if we have low expectations we also will be successful.) Second, we need to share our expectations, if for no other reason than to check if they are sufficient and defensible. This means we need to share our conceptions of what impact means, how we would know if this impact is realized in student learning, provide exemplars of what this impact looks like, and critique our beliefs about the magnitude of this impact – together.

Eells provided a powerful example:

> If the collective activity consists of the sum of independent successes, as it does for a track and field team, then it is preferable to measure and aggregate the personal efficacies of the actors. When an entire group must interact, like a basketball team would, and collective activity is the product of cooperative work, then it makes more sense to measure group members' beliefs about what the team can accomplish.
>
> (p. 66)

In schools, collective efficacy is very influenced by school organizational features such as responsiveness of administrators to encouraging teacher collaboration. If, however, we allow conversations to dwell on the insurmountable difficulties of educating students (their post code, their parents, their lack of motivation, their lack of preparedness), then we are very likely to undermine teachers' sense of efficacy. In schools where teachers work together to find ways to address the learning, motivation, and behavior problems, students are the major beneficiaries.

The narrative in a school should be less about "how to teach" and more about the "impact of teaching." What does it mean to be "good at year 5 English," what does it mean to grow at least a year in year 8 sports coaching? What evidence of impact on student work, and on how students think about their work, would convince us that this is a year's growth? There are no easy answers, but it is with the collective dialogue and then the sense of confidence that we can all realize these levels of impact that make the greatest difference to the outcomes for students. It is also unlikely to be one source – it needs triangulation across test scores, artifacts from lessons, observations of students, and listening to their voice about their learning.

We see nine steps toward the development of collective efficacy and endorsing the mindframe "I collaborate with my peers and my students about my conceptions of progress and my impact." First, an understanding that "I cause learning." Second, the importance of high expectations for all students and agreeing that "we are jointly responsible for each student." Third, evaluative thinking which relates to seeking to evaluate the impact of my teaching. Fourth, having the "I" skills (I am self-aware, I am a learner about my impact, I can manage conflict and queries about my impact) and the "we" skills (I have high levels of social sensitivity, I wish to have a shared purpose to improve, I am prepared to problem solve, I trust and respect the views of others). Fifth, I work with others to seek evidence of impact to feed and justify our high levels of confidence to make the difference that matters. Sixth, I can work with others to agree on the sufficient and high levels of growth we aim to achieve over this school year. Seventh, I am prepared to focus on excellent diagnosis of what the students bring to the class, how they undertake their learning, and the impact I have on these students. Eighth, I work and evaluate together with my colleagues to have a common conception of progress and a joy in the high positive impact we are having, and to continue to work together on maximizing this impact. All this depends on the ninth step, the role of school leaders to legitimate, support, esteem, and create the trust and time needed to develop collective efficacy.

Micro-teaching

Micro-teaching refers to methods for planning small-scale lessons in a group and analyzing and discussing them with the help of videos (see Figure 3.1). It can be expanded to viewing videos of teachers in their usual classrooms. This provides an under-the-microscope view of teaching practices and teaching behavior, but more important, it can allow discussion about the impact of teachers on the students. The effect size of 0.88 this factor achieves testifies to its effectiveness. But we make a critical distinction between using micro-teaching to watch a teacher teach and to watch the impact of a teacher teaching. It is primarily the latter that makes the difference. It can also help to invite a teacher to "think aloud" as they watch themselves teach (especially when the audio is turned off) to hear their mindframes and the moment-by-moment decisions that they claim to have made. It is less the technology of "micro-teaching" but the opportunity to hear the thinking of teachers, to see their impact on students, and to create a common dialogue about thinking and impact.

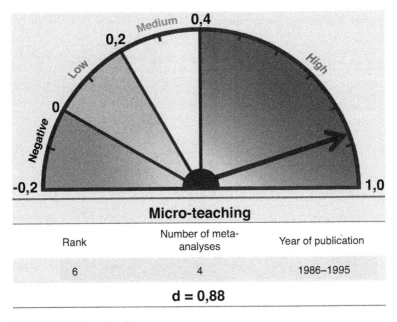

Micro-teaching

Rank	Number of meta-analyses	Year of publication
6	4	1986–1995

d = 0,88

FIGURE 3.1 Micro-teaching

Source: Hattie and Zierer (2017).

Professional development

"Professional development" achieves a large effect size (d = 0.62) in Visible Learning – although it is also one of the more variable influences (see Figure 3.2). That is, not every further training and continuing education program for teachers is successful. Rather, successful professional development programs are characterized by working together to understand, enhance, and evaluate the impact of teachers on their students. Once again, it is the collaborative nature of the learning that makes the difference. Although it needs to be noted that when the aim of professional development is specific to individuals' learning needs, this collaboration may be less critical, but when the aim of professional development is arranged at a school level, then the collaboration is the essence. In this latter case, there needs to be active school leadership; often, external expertise is needed to ensure commitment and impact from the professional development, and there needs to be a needs analysis to ensure not only that the professional development is appropriately chosen but also serves as baseline to then subsequently evaluate the impact of the professional development.

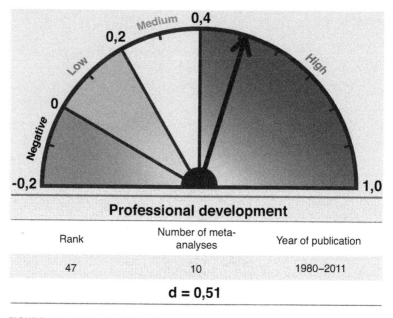

Professional development

Rank	Number of meta-analyses	Year of publication
47	10	1980–2011

d = 0,51

FIGURE 3.2 Professional development

Source: Hattie and Zierer (2017).

As in every other learning process, feedback is one of the key factors of professional development. Feedback given to teachers in this context should not be focused only at the levels of the task and the process but also and especially at the level of self-regulation. Teachers profit greatly from professional development if it provides them with concrete goals and steps for improving and evaluating their instruction in the future. Just as important, the participants should receive an opportunity to give feedback on axe professional development measure so it can be adjusted to fit their learning level.

Collective intelligence as a product of exchange and cooperation

Every one of us knows what a computer mouse is and how to use one, but only few of us know how they work, and even less of us know how they are constructed – and, to take this example even further, most of us are not capable of building all the necessary parts ourselves and assembling a working mouse out of them. The complex task this seemingly so ordinary object performs is possible only thanks to the exchange and cooperation of many people. The technological advances that went into developing the computer mouse include progress in the production of raw materials, the plastics industry and, not least, programming.

One might be inclined to object that this form of exchange and cooperation applies only to complex objects, but consider a pencil – a writing instrument that has a much longer history than a computer mouse and seems much less complex. Yet in this case as well it is doubtful that one person alone would be capable of chopping down a tree, drying out and cutting the wood, shaping the lead, and finally combining the wood and the lead to form a pencil. In a word, the production of a pencil also involves exchange and cooperation.

Social scientists use the term "collective intelligence" to gain insight into these relationships. The term goes all the way back to antiquity. Aristotle refers to the idea in his so-called summation argument, and attributed to the Greek philosopher is the notion that the whole is greater than the sum of its parts. In our own times, Matt Ridley achieved a great deal of notoriety in this connection with his book *The Rational Optimist* (2010). He presents numerous examples of the possibilities and opportunities associated with collective intelligence, including those described in the vignette at the start of this chapter. Ultimately, he even sees collective intelligence as the key feature of successful cultures, institutions, and people, because all less successful cultures, institutions, and people are not open, do not exchange ideas and goods, and therefore do not work together in this regard. Isolation means stagnation and leads in the long term even to regression.

We teachers have always had an ambivalent relationship with exchange and cooperation: On the one hand, we demand cooperation of our students every day and regard them as important values for education. On the other hand, although we experience in the course of our own education how to bring learners to discuss and cooperate with each other, we receive only little support in learning these skills ourselves but are largely on our own in this important task. In addition, many teachers are even socialized to be lone wolves in the early stage of their education, where the most important things are good grades, the best performances, and the most convincing demonstration lessons. Why should we make our own ideas, materials, and lesson plans available to others? It is not rare to hear of teachers who regard exchange and cooperation with colleagues as hardly more than a waste of time, because the others chip in so little and they themselves work just as well and just as fast on their own. Moreover, my classroom is my private domain. We think of some colleagues as "social loafers" who sit back, barely engage, but run off with the credit based on the work of the others in a group. This might be true in individual cases, but as a blanket statement it is not always true. To demonstrate this point, Matt Ridley cites the following example, which focuses only on the aspect of time but still serves to illustrate the power of exchange and cooperation (cf. Ridley, 2010).

Both Adam and Oz can make spears and axes. Whereas Adam needs four hours to make a spear and three hours to make an ax, Oz can make a spear in one hour and an ax in two hours. If they each need to make one spear and one axe, Adam needs seven hours and Oz only three hours to complete the job.

	Adam	Oz
Spear	4	1
Axe	3	2
Total	7	3

What happens if the two work together? At first, it might seem to make little sense for Oz, because he will not save any time by working together with Adam on two spears and two axes. But what if they divide up the work as follows? Oz uses his strength to make two spears in two hours. In return, Adam uses his strength to make two axes in six hours. They then exchange a spear and an ax. In this case, both Adam and Oz need to invest one hour less than if they were working alone to obtain a spear and an ax.

	Adam	Oz
2 spears	0	2
2 axes	6	0
	Exchange of spear and axe	
Total	6	2

Exchange and cooperation clearly benefit both sides – even though we are neglecting the fact that it is possible to make a spear or an ax better or worse. Still, saving time in this way alone is already a form of collective intelligence, and the benefits only increase as tasks to be completed become more complex.

What if we replaced the spear with a worksheet and the ax with a test? Or, to take this example even further, what if we replaced the spear and the ax with ideas for designing a lesson, experience evaluating instruction, feedback, goal formulation, teacher-student relationships, motivation, practice, differentiation, classroom management, and so forth? The benefit of collective intelligence in these cases is not just temporal in nature but consists above all in the power of dialogue, in the strength of exchange and cooperation, and in professional development in a team. All of this is more than a mere exchange of information, an act of collecting things and filing them away. Collective intelligence becomes visible in intensive, constructive, and concentrated discussions about one's own competencies and mindframes.

It is time to develop a culture of exchange and cooperation in our schools so that we can harness the power of collective intelligence to the benefit of learners and also to the benefit of teachers.

Team teaching: possibilities and limits of a seemingly self-evident factor

One of the criticisms of "I collaborate with my peers and my students about my conceptions of progress and my impact" is the lowly place of "co-/teaching" in Visible Learning. The factor "co-/team teaching" is only 118th place with an effect size of 0.19 and thus falls far short of expectations for many. How can this be? How can team teaching have such a low effect when implementing it involves making great concessions and shouldering immense costs? The factor "co-/team teaching" demonstrates yet again that understanding why a factor is unsuccessful is the basis for improving its effectiveness in the future. How, then, are we to understand the low effect size of team teaching?

An anecdote might help to answer this question: Experts in Austria recommended introducing team teaching in inclusive classes to meet the additional educational and instructional challenge such classes clearly pose. It was no sooner said than done: Inclusive classes were provided with two teachers each. Some time later, it was possible to observe an interesting development in the relationship between the teachers. They had come up with a special name for the second teacher in the classroom: the "radiator teacher." Why? Because this teacher leaned on the radiator while the other teacher taught. And when the first teacher was finished teaching, she would go over to the radiator and hand over responsibility for the class to her colleague.

This is at best parallel "single teaching" and misses the power of team teaching.

The teaching described in the anecdote is not team teaching, because the teachers do not teach *with* one another but *after* one another. And as long as team teaching consists of nothing other than this, its effect cannot be much larger than as if one teacher was teaching at a time (the typical class experience). Rather, team teaching demands that the teachers possess a special competence and a special mindframe, because delivering instruction is a highly complex activity that loses nothing of its complexity just because it is being done in pairs. This complexity demands that teachers working together possess several abilities: analyzing the learners' initial learning levels together, setting and formulating instructional goals together, designing tasks together and differentiating them as necessary, delivering the lesson together, and finally, evaluating the lesson together. And they probably need high levels of social sensitivity to each other, a listening ability, and the competence to build high levels of trust. All of this is not easy. On top of this, planning, delivering, and evaluating a lesson demands more than just competencies. It also requires a number of mindframes: the mindframe to make a mistake before one's colleague, to make compromises, to restrain oneself and hold back one's own ideas and preferences, to be ready to assume responsibility for tasks that one is perhaps not particularly good at, or to have the courage to try something out that involves relying on a colleague. These mindframes are unfortunately not (yet) taught deliberately and systematically in teacher education programs. Too many younger teachers desire to just have their own classrooms – just leave me alone in my class, let me create resources, do my own marking. No wonder after a few years of such busy work they feel "not supported." This notion of the "good teacher" as a resource developer, a marker of students work, and a king or queen of his or her own domain mitigates against cooperation with other teachers about their conceptions of impact and progress and is a major impediment to teaching becoming a profession – the students are the losers if this is the mindframe.

Consequently, team teaching demands a high degree of competencies and mindframes. Successful team teaching as a form of collective intelligence does not just appear all on its own accord. It requires exchange and cooperation and thus also competence and mindframes on the part of the teachers. And when it is truly cooperative and focused on jointly maximizing the collective impact, then it leads to a much higher impact on students.

Where can I start?

The research findings discussed earlier demonstrate one thing clearly: The necessary competence and mindframe for successful cooperation, exchange, and cooperation need to be learned. Against this backdrop, a good place to start working on the mindframe "I collaborate" is to first become conscious of your own behavior about exchange and cooperation and then use this knowledge to identify the fields in which more cooperation can have a lasting positive effect. The following list can be useful for this reflection. It attempts to identify various levels of cooperation and arrange them in order of difficulty:

Steps of cooperation

1. Discussing with one another.
2. Supporting and criticizing one other.
3. Planning and evaluating lessons together.
4. Delivering lessons together.

This sequence of steps is based on the insight that it is easier to discuss general criteria of instruction than to support and criticize one another's concrete ideas for a lesson, and both steps are easier than planning and evaluating lessons together. The crowning point of cooperation between teachers is then delivering lessons together and evaluating the impact of these lessons on students together – particularly as this represents the consummation of all the teamwork and therefore involves bringing together not just the thinking but also the action of the team members.

The core skill is working together on what are agreed success criteria, what is the current diagnosis of what the students know and are able to do, and whether the planned intervention is highly likely to move the students from where they are to where we all want them to be. It is this joint discussion about appropriate criteria of success and the expected levels of growth over the course of the lessons that matters the most.

In light of these considerations, we would like to warn against an overly hasty implementation of team teaching. You should proceed to this step of exchange and cooperation only once you have begun to develop the necessary competencies (including high levels of trust and social sensitivity) and mindframes. As an initial step, we recommend discussing with your colleagues about what you expect in terms of student growth. A good way of doing so is to consider the following table of factors from Visible Learning, assess their effectiveness based on your own teaching experience, and then discuss them with a colleague. You will find that your opinions will often differ, and so will your understanding of the factors as such. But these are precisely the discussions teachers need to have to exchange ideas about their thinking and actions and cooperate as educational experts:

	Negative	Low	Medium	High
Class size	O	O	O	O
Open vs. traditional	O	O	O	O
Audio visual methods	O	O	O	O
Subject matter knowledge	O	O	O	O
Piagetian programs	O	O	O	O
Goals	O	O	O	O
Spaced vs. massed practice	O	O	O	O
Teacher-student relationship	O	O	O	O
Cooperative learning	O	O	O	O
Direct instruction	O	O	O	O
Socio-economic status	O	O	O	O
Motivation	O	O	O	O
Feedback	O	O	O	O
Formative evaluation	O	O	O	O
Co-Teaching/Team-Teaching	O	O	O	O

The next step of cooperation might be to work together on the mindframe "I am a change agent." Take, for example, the ARCS model of motivation described in the following chapter of this book, in which we already touched on the importance of motivation, in introducing a lesson. Another of the greatest challenges for teachers is to learn how to steer their pedagogical creativity in a direction that wins learners over for the topic and captures their attention at the beginning of the lesson. Teachers experience how difficult this is day in and day out, and their attempts are not always successful. It is, therefore, more than surprising that hardly any schools have launched an attempt to collect and share effective introductions to instructional sequences among their teachers. Instead, everyone tries their hand at this crucial task alone. So why not pool your pedagogical creativity? Take the ARCS model and try to collect as many motivational strategies as you can, reflect on them, and discuss them with your colleagues, particularly in regard to their effectiveness and your experiences applying them. For instance, you might note what to consider in selecting media, how the learners reacted to the strategy you applied, where there was a lack of clarity, and what the learners suggested as means of improvement. This process of searching for evidence for one's own thinking and action in instruction is clearly connected with the mindframe "I am an evaluator of my impact on student learning," because the only people who can provide a meaningful answer to these questions are the students.

The examples cited earlier demonstrate the main idea of cooperation as emphasized again and again in Visible Learning: Know thy impact. What this means is that exchange and cooperation between teachers should focus on questioning instruction to gauge its effectiveness and search for evidence. The purpose of cooperation is thus not to accumulate an arsenal of material, to characterize learners, to diagnose parents, or to stigmatize colleagues, but to scrutinize one's own thinking and action about teaching and while teaching and to ask the questions: What is not effective? and Why not? But also, What is effective? and Why? The latter questions are particularly important, above all in regard to job satisfaction: knowing that one is a successful teacher and why.

It will, of course, not be necessary to reach the last step of cooperation in all fields and at all times. Rather, the list introduced earlier is intended as a guide to ensure that one does not go too fast and thus overload the sensitive field of cooperation. This sensitivity is reflected in the fundamental mindframes involved: Cooperation demands certain mindframes, especially confidence and trust. Otto von Bismarck, known to history as the first Chancellor of Germany, called attention to this point with the following words: "Confidence is a tender plant. Once it is destroyed, it does not come back again so quickly."

CHECKLIST

Reflect on the following points next time you plan a lesson:

- Know that educational expertise involves cooperation.
- Exchange ideas with your colleagues and discuss instruction.
- Reduce your workload by sharing responsibility.

■ Start with general questions and apply them step by step to a concrete lesson.

■ Take a look at instructional material together, for instance worksheets, chalkboard drawings, or assignments.

■ Always take student achievements as a basis for justifying your exchange and your cooperation.

■ Search for evidence in cooperating with your colleagues.

■ Reflect on your instruction as well as your cooperation in regard to your competence and mindframe.

EXERCISES

■ Go back to the questionnaire for self-reflection at the start of the chapter and complete it again in a different color. Where and, more important, why has your perspective on the statements changed? Discuss your self-assessment with a colleague.

■ Show a colleague the introduction to one of your lessons, a worksheet, a chalkboard drawing, a video sequence, or another instructional aid and ask him or her whether it lacks clarity in any regard. Meet with your colleague again after giving the lesson to discuss how the learners experienced it.

■ Present to a colleague the goal you formulated for a lesson, the tasks you gave the learners, and how they completed them. Take their achievements as a basis for discussing how well the goals fit the various achievement levels, how clearly the tasks were presented, and what form they were presented in.

I am a change agent and believe all students can improve

QUESTIONNAIRE FOR SELF-REFLECTION

Assess yourself by rating your agreement with the following statements: 1 = strongly disagree, 5 = strongly agree.

I am very good at . . .

applying successful methods to make my teaching more differentiated.

applying various strategies for enhancing the students' motivation.

I know perfectly well . . .

that my teaching has an impact on the students.

that there are various strategies for enhancing motivation.

My goal is always to . . .

have an impact on the students through my teaching.

motivate the students in their learning process.

I am thoroughly convinced . . .

of having a positive impact on the students through my teaching.

that it is important to continuously question the impact of my teaching.

VIGNETTE

Consider the following situation – perhaps it even reminds you of something from your own childhood: A highly motivated and interested learner decides he wants to explore a new field of knowledge, but what he hears from his parents is, "You can't do it. It's too difficult." The success of the endeavor hangs in the balance: Will the learner succeed in convincing his parents that they are wrong? Does he have the strength? Or will he believe the people around him and suppress his own interests and motivations to their opinions? How different the same learner's learning process can be when he hears the words, "You can do it. We believe in you." His interest will grow, and his motivation will increase, unleashing powers he never knew he had in him. Faith really can move mountains.

What is this chapter about?

This vignette illustrates this chapter's main message: Learning has a lot to do with perspectives – particularly on the perspective of the teacher and its impact on the learner's motivation, the perspective of the parents and its impact on the learner's confidence, the perspective of the peers and their impact on learner's engagement, and the perspective of the learners themselves and its impact on their ability to see themselves as consumers or producers of their own learning. If the student is not learning, it is because we have not yet found the strategy to make learning happen. Successful learning requires targeted perspectives, and it is the responsibility of all around the learner (teachers, parents, peers) to build up, support, and develop positive perspectives in all involved. This necessarily involves seeing oneself as a change agent.

When you finish reading this chapter, you should be able to take this message as a basis for explaining:

- how significant the factors "classroom management," "advance organizers," and "problem-based learning" are.
- what influence motivation has on learning and what possibilities teachers have to motivate students.
- why you should select appropriate strategies to support student learning based on both the evidence that they will work and your knowledge about what a student might need.

■ that it is not necessary to convince everyone completely of your own ideas. Rather, it is enough to win over a critical mass for your vision.

Which factors from Visible Learning support this mindframe?

As stressful as political election campaigns may be, they are very instructive from a social scientific perspective. For example, consider this poster from Barack Obama's presidential campaign and think about what associations it evokes for you (see Figure 4.1; cf. https://wpshout.com/change-wordpress-theme-external-php/).

FIGURE 4.1 Change what you see

Hardly anyone will have negative emotions when looking at this poster. The message is positive through and through: Change is possible. It is up to you what you make out of your life. It makes you the core agent of what can change. It implies that you can be successful. Accordingly, the slogan of the election campaign was "Yes we can."

Aiming for students to have agency in their learning is indeed a major aim in learning, but this does not mean we leave them alone; rather, ask them to take control over their learning, but work with them in gaining this agency – which includes asking for help, seeking to find out what they do not know, and working beyond what they can do now.

One of the above average effects relate to Outward Bound Adventure courses. Why would kayaking down a white river or abseiling down a cliff lead to increases in mathematics and reading? We spent 10 years working with Outward Bound to understand this effect. If you have never kayaked and on the first bend of the river get into trouble, you do not have control over learning, you do not have the time to problem solve, you do not know enough to resolve the problem – you need to know how to ask for help, quickly and convincingly. Similarly, when confronting issues in schooling, we need to know how to ask for help, the climate of trust needs to be high to allow for the help to be asked and heard, you need to be put in situations where you are challenged to make mistakes (out of your zone of comfort), and there must be help there to resolve the dilemma – and then off you paddle to the next wave. This creates a "yes we can" mindset to learning in a situation when we most rapidly need to learn and ask for help to learn.

Growth mindset was developed by Carol Dweck from a lifetime of careful and precise research work. She claimed that growth mindsets can inspire different goals and shape views about effort, but she has never claimed in her academic writings that there is a state of mind called "growth mindset" – it is not an attribute of a person, rather, it is a way of thinking in a particular circumstance. She has undertaken many research studies to understand when and where it can be invoked to lead to better outcomes. It is a more a coping strategy than a state of being.

The "particular circumstance" is when we do not know an answer, when we make an error, when we experience failure, when we are anxious, or when we do not know what to do next. Note, for example, some of Dweck's claims:

> Growth mindset leads to expending more empathetic effort in contexts where empathy is challenging (e.g., when they disagree with someone or some other they do not know is suffering)
>
> (Murphy & Dweck, 2016, p. 487)

> In situations when students are over confident – they allocated less time to difficult problems
>
> (2016, p. 98)

> The triggers for when growth matters: When we face challenge; Receive criticism, or fare poorly compared with others; When threatened or defensive
>
> (Dweck, 2015, pp. 3–4)

> Peer conflict and peer exclusion
>
> (Yeager & Dweck, 2012, p. 309)

> When we make mistakes or reveal deficiencies, try to hide mistakes, feel we do not have the ability
>
> (Dweck, 2017)

> Those who see "failure-is-debilitating" as opposed to those who see "failure-is-enhancing."
>
> (Haimovitz & Dweck, 2016, p. 866)

The key question is, "*When* is the appropriate situation for thinking in a growth manner over a fixed manner?" In these situations, having access to growth thinking helps resolve the situation, move the person forward, and not lead to resistance, overreaction, and fear of flight into a fixed mindset.

Most recently, Dweck (2017) noted her research relates directly to how students perceive their abilities – which has a long history via terms such as "self-attribution," "locus of control," "calibration," and many other related notions. She brought a sharpness to two of the core ideas – the belief that one's intelligence or abilities can be changed or that it is fixed and immutable. Like all good researchers, she noted that she continues to learn more about how these processes are working, can be enhanced, and can be misused. For example, she states that a growth mindset is not merely about effort, praise, feeling good, having a positive outlook, believing everyone is smart, or used to explain why some students are not learning ("Oh, he has a fixed mindset."). They should not be used to personify that the student alone is responsible for learning or not learning; should not be used to classify students into either a growth or fixed mindset category; should not assume growth mindset is about praising and rewarding effort; and should not inculcate growth mindset by focusing on positive mission statements, "I can" posters, and students mouthing platitudes about growth as though that would lead to good things happening.

Indeed, we need to delve more deeply about the reasons for learning or not learning; there needs to be evidence of when to use the growth and fixed notions in the practice as well as language of the classroom. Too often, an adult will endorse the claims of "growth" in their words but not in their actions and particular reactions to children's mistakes. Dweck notes we are all a mixture of growth and fixed notions and need to understand both in ourselves. The current meta-analysis of growth programs show very low effect sizes, primarily because most programs are not what Dweck was claiming, and because changing fixed into growth mindsets for the right occasions is very difficult.

Getting people to pursue an appropriately challenging goal, motivating them, and appealing to their emotions are important abilities to have if one wishes to change people. This is not just a problem for politicians but is also a challenge faced by many teachers every day in the classroom: How is it possible to convince learners to tackle a more difficult problem, fill them with enthusiasm, and inspire them? Every teacher knows that this is no easy task. It is also a task that is becoming more complex as society becomes more diverse and as there are more distractions to tempt interests, prior knowledge, and previous experiences. This means that teachers need to be change agents. Visible Learning contains a number of factors to back up this claim. We describe a few of them in the following.

Setting the conditions: classroom management

With an effect size of 0.52, "classroom management" is one of the most influential factors with an extensive research history (see Figure 4.2). Good classroom management is a scene-setter for trust to

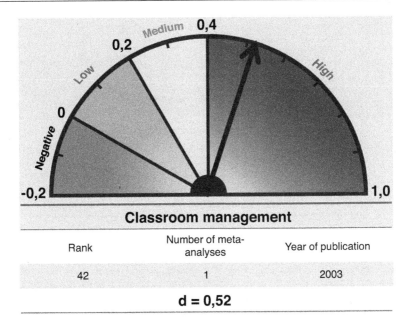

Classroom management

Rank	Number of meta-analyses	Year of publication
42	1	2003

d = 0,52

FIGURE 4.2 Classroom management

Source: Hattie and Zierer (2017).

be built, for fairness to be dominant, and for learning to then occur. Preventive strategies are a more effective means of dealing with disruptive behavior in the classroom than reprimands and punishment. This idea becomes visible in the following classroom management strategies, which have been developed out of the various research findings on this issue.

Focus and presence	Signal to the learners that you are present in the classroom and that you notice even little things. Do not devote your entire attention to disturbances immediately. Instead, remain focused primarily on your lesson and try to address the disturbance at the same time, for instance with non-verbal signals.
Smoothness and pace	Avoid idle time and a loss of pace in your lesson, because they cause minds to wander and often lead to classroom disruptions. This involves implementing a number of rules and rituals, work formats, and behavioral patterns together with the students.
Group focus	Try as often as you can to address all learners at the same time. If you have to speak to a group at length, give the rest of the learners a task to keep them engaged in learning.

(Continued)

Avoidance of tedium	Classroom disturbances can usually be avoided when the students experience the lesson as stimulating and interesting, as informative and fun. Note, boredom is the effect size with the most negative impact. The most effective strategy is to engage them in appropriately challenging learning and make them aware of their incremental successes in learning, which invites them back into the learning. A way to do this is to include situations in which the learners experience success situations (which can include learning from errors) and to avoid offending or embarrassing students and assigning tasks that are too challenging or too boring for them.

The key thing to remember in this context is that successful classroom management involves not just competence but also an appropriate mindframe: Is your goal to avoid disruptive behavior in the first place by taking preventive measures, or is your goal to react to disruptive behavior by imposing punishments? Although you may switch between these two goals from one minute to the next in the classroom, your perspective of your own role as a teacher differs in each case: In the first case, you see yourself as a change agent on behalf of the learners whose job is to initiate interactions in the classroom, whereas in the second case, you are merely reacting to these interactions.

Provide success criteria for the learning

So much has been written about devising criteria of success for a series of lessons. We work on (about) a 6–10-week cycle to outline what success looks like. This can be accomplished by providing examples of A, B, and C work, by experiencing up front (not necessarily on day 1) an assessment appropriate to the end of series, by talking with students who have already mastered the success criteria, and by working with the students to co-construct the criteria of success. Another way to help understand the notions of success is to be more specific about the learning intentions during the cycle of lessons leading to the success criteria. The key is that learning intentions without success criteria have a much lower effect; learning intentions are the more specific ways of getting to the notions of success. By themselves, learning intentions can become disjointed, too surface level, and too jingoistic, and so often they are not about the learning but too much about the doing. It is not, what are we doing today? It is, what are we learning today? And how would we know when we get there?

Advance organizers

Advance organizers are one method for establishing a link between existing knowledge and new information and for defining and organizing the most important phases of upcoming instruction treating this new material. The effect size of 0.41 they achieve in Visible Learning may be regarded as average, and if they were combined with success criteria, this effect increases (see Figure 4.3).

As the results of the meta-analyses show great variation, however, it is necessary to ask about criteria for applying advance organizers successfully. Two aspects are important: First, advance organizers are generally more effective when they not only address surface understanding but also take into account deep understanding – recall, it is the appropriate proportion of surface to deep that matters most. Second, advance organizers achieve greater effects when they are made available to the learners and not used just as a tool to plan lessons. These two aspects enable the teacher to show the students the significance of prior knowledge and experience, make the criteria for success in the upcoming learning process visible to them, and reach an understanding with them on these criteria. This is a key advantage of advance organizers: They imply a change in the way learners understand their role in the learning process,

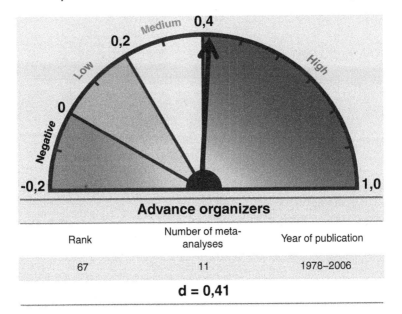

Rank	Number of meta-analyses	Year of publication
67	11	1978–2006

d = 0,41

FIGURE 4.3 Advance organizer

Source: Hattie and Zierer (2017).

away from passiveness and toward action and personal responsibility. This can happen only if teachers see themselves as change agents. Figure 4.3 above is an example of an advance organizer.

Our topic

What do I already know?

What do I need to learn?

What are the gaps between what I now know and what I need to know?

What can I do to reduce this gap?

Problem-based learning

"Problem-based learning," a method that involves using a problem to present learning material, originated in the tradition of focusing instruction more strongly toward the learner. Although the effect size of 0.15 calculated in Visible Learning is low, the research findings on this factor are interesting for the mindframe "See yourself as a change agent.": The meta-analyses demonstrate that problem-based learning can indeed have a great impact on student performance if it is

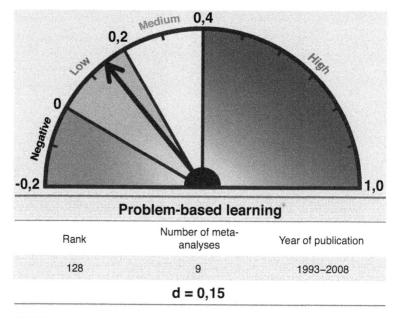

Rank	Number of meta-analyses	Year of publication
128	9	1993–2008

d = 0,15

FIGURE 4.4 Problem-based learning

Source: Hattie and Zierer (2017).

implemented at the right time in the learning process (see Figure 4.4). The right time is not while the students are still in the domain of surface understanding, where problem-based learning can even have a negative effect, but once they have reached the domain of deep understanding. In other words, problem-based learning will have an effect only if the learners have already acquired the necessary knowledge base to complete tasks at the levels of transfer and problem solving. In addition, it requires that the teachers possess not only the competence to identify the learning levels of the students at the start and then assign them appropriate problems but also the right mindframes to lead the learners into the domain of deep understanding and motivate them to work on the problems. Focusing on problems is undoubtedly an exceptional approach from a pedagogical standpoint, because it has fundamental effects on building a positive culture of mistakes, being a valuable part of feedback process, as well as on learners' self-regulation, and on possibilities for dividing up the class into groups. Whether problem-based learning is effective, therefore, depends on several aspects, and it is one of many methods teachers can implement on the basis of evidence.

The factors "classroom management," "advance organizers," and "problem-based learning" indicate how influential the perspective of the teacher is for his or her thinking and actions in the classroom. Just as important as what teachers see is how they see it and what beliefs and judgments they are guided by. The teacher's own perspective on learning and teaching thus has lasting effects on the success of children and youths in school.

Learners need to be motivated

In view of the research findings on the influence of motivation on learning, the effect size of 0.48 for "motivation" in Visible Learning comes as little surprise: Learning requires motivation, and it is difficult to initiate learning processes without motivation. At first glance, it might seem unimportant whether this motivation is internal (intrinsic) or external (extrinsic), because the learner will try hard in both cases. When one takes a closer look at these two forms of motivation, however, one notices an important difference in regard to learning intensity and retention: Whereas extrinsically motivated learning often remains in the domain of surface understanding and leads only to short-term learning gains, intrinsically motivated learning leads to deep understanding and enables long-term learning gains. Intrinsic motivation is, therefore, preferable to extrinsic motivation.

Teachers can frame this issue in psychological terms and ask: How can I promote intrinsic motivation in my students? Or they can approach it from a methodological standpoint and consider: What possibilities are available for motivating my students? Every teacher knows that these are not easy questions to answer. As soon as one enters the classroom, it is clear from the facial expressions and body language of many of the learners whether they will show interest in what is to come. In the latter case, teachers have two options open to them: Either they can take this indifference as a given and resign themselves to the fact that these students will be lost for the entire instructional sequence, or they can question themselves and their teaching and reconsider the possibilities for motivating these students in order to hopefully arouse their interest in the lesson after all. It goes without saying that this decision is a matter of having the right mindframe and that the second option will be more successful. It is the teachers' responsibility to set the tone in the class and to motivate students, not vice versa.

Incidentally, the same thing goes for situations in which the motivational strategy one chooses turns out to be unsuccessful. Again, teachers have two options for dealing with the situation: Either they can argue that the learners did not understand things again and take consolation in the belief that they did all they could, or they can search for new strategies, regard the learners' failure as their own failure, and thus take it as a challenge.

Empirical educational research offers several practical models to help teachers meet this challenge, to see themselves as change agents again and again and act accordingly. These models endeavor to bring together methods that have been shown to have a positive effect on student learning. One useful model for motivating students is the ARCS model by John Keller (2010) (see Figure 4.5).

This model distinguishes between four categories of motivation that teachers can influence by applying corresponding motivational strategies:

- Strategies for generating attention include generating a conflict between prior knowledge and an observation, using humor, or giving the students the chance to ask questions.
- Strategies for generating relevance include highlighting the current or future importance of a lesson's topic.
- Strategies for generating confidence include presenting tasks that learners are (only just) capable of completing or strengthening their self-confidence.

	Perceptual Arousal	Inquiry Arousal	Variability
Attention	Provide novelty and surprise	Stimulate curiosity by posing questions or problems to solve	Incorporate a range of methods and media to meet students' varying needs
	Goal Orientation	**Motive Matching**	**Familiarity**
Relevance	Present objectives and useful purpose of instruction and specific methods for successful achievement	Match objectives to student needs and motives	Present content in ways that are understandable and that are related to the learners' experiences and values
	Learning Requirements	**Successful Opportunities**	**Personal Responsibility**
Confidence	Inform students about learning and performance requirements and assessment criteria	Provide challenging and meaningful opportunities for successful learning	Link learning success to students' personal effort and ability
	Intrinsic Reinforcement	**Extrinsic Rewards**	**Equity**
Satisfaction	Encourage and support intrinsic enjoyment of the learning experience	Provide positive reinforcement and motivational feedback	Maintain consistent standards and consequences for success

FIGURE 4.5 ARCS model

Source: Keller (2010)

- Strategies for generating satisfaction include strengthening positive developments or unexpectedly giving students recognition for an achievement.

It is not possible to reach every learner with the same motivational strategy, because existing motivation can vary. This means that it is necessary to apply a variety of methods. But try not to get carried away.

Against variety for variety's sake: a call for an evidence-based variety of methods

There is a widespread belief that a good lesson is a lesson that goes off without a hitch and keeps the learners busy as long as possible through the use of as many different methods as possible. Lessons like this certainly appear ordered and structured, but that does not make them good lessons. Just because the learners were engaged in prolonged activity does not mean they used the learning time effectively, and just because a well-coordinated variety of methods was used does not mean all the learning goals were achieved. As an illustration of this point, consider the following anecdote from teacher education. Such situations are unfortunately not a thing of the past but still happen today.

Many trainee teachers are asked to give demonstration lessons involving individual, partner, and group work and featuring a teacher lecture, a student presentation, and a class discussion. If the trainee succeeds in smoothly integrating all these elements into the lesson – which, to be ironic about it, generally is the case if the students were coached to play their roles correctly beforehand – then he or she receives a perfect grade, on the grounds that the lesson integrated a wide range of methods.

However, the emphasis is placed on the wrong aspect in this example: Much more important than the diversity of the methods the teacher applied is how successful these methods were and whether they achieved their goal. The key issue in demonstration lessons should actually be, first, whether the methods used in the lesson helped to achieve the learning goals and, second, whether the trainee teacher demonstrated this and provided empirical evidence for it in the lesson. This makes evidence the criterion for selecting a method, confirming in practice Wolfgang Klafki's (1996) theoretical assumption that didactics should take precedence over methodology.

This perspective also makes it clear that there is no single best teaching method. It is less a matter of advocating a particular method of teaching and more of asking about the impact of the teaching that was used, and if it was not changing the method of teaching to then attain the success criteria of the lesson. If, for example, the teacher did not succeed in getting the learners to achieve the learning goals despite having implemented a brilliantly well-thought-out and creative learning arrangement, then it was not a good lesson. If the teacher succeeded in leading all the students to success with a monotonous lesson, on the other hand, then it was a good lesson. These conditions can, of course, also appear in the reverse order.

However, the following consideration shows why it can still make sense to require trainee teachers to use as many methods as possible in their demonstration lessons: It is relatively easy to show that one has applied a single method successfully, but it takes a good deal of professionalism to provide evidence for the success of many methods applied in various steps of the instructional process.

We, therefore, recommend applying a variety of evidence-based methods: A variety of methods is necessary even just due to the differences in the students' learning levels at the start of the lesson. At the same time, however, this "diversity of minds," as Johann Friedrich Herbart (1808) terms it, also demands that one examine which methods were implemented successfully and which were not – in order to make evidence-based decisions in the further course of the instructional sequence.

Applying methods on the basis of evidence does not require an additional, highly standardized, and scientific data collection procedure – there are enough data available already, and one would be well advised in many cases to make good use of the data one already has before conducting new studies. Rather, evidence in this context means existing data a teacher collects during regular school days: observation of group work, the completion of a worksheet, or things said by learners or in conferences with their parents, to name just a few examples. Analyzing the effects of this data, relating it to one's own thinking and actions, and drawing on empirical research findings to support one's decision making are the crucial elements of the evidence-based approach to methods recommended in Visible Learning. It is hence not a matter of collecting more data but of looking at the available data in another way.

Critical mass: on the conditions for successful change

Principals frequently ask themselves how much of the teaching staff they need to win over to implement a certain reform. Similarly, teachers ask themselves again and again how much support they need from their learners to successfully initiate a learning process. The answer to these questions one often hears is: 100 percent.

Apart from the fact that this answer places those involved under an enormous amount of pressure, it is also incorrect: Research findings from economics (cf. Endres & Martiensen, 2007) show that it can be enough for a company that wants to achieve a monopoly over a market to start with a share of not 100, not 50, but just 20 to 30 percent. This demonstrates that getting changes underway involves reaching a critical mass.

Game theorists speak in this connection of a threshold. Once it has been reached, a development is set in motion without any further intervention, reforming the system and replacing it with a new one. Studies have shown that this effect is particularly common in group-dynamic processes and is thus relevant for all forms of leadership and management.

Consequently, it will be enough for principals to convince a critical mass of teachers of their vision to translate it successfully into action, and it will be enough for teachers to arouse a critical mass of interest and motivation in their learners to initiate a learning process. There is no overall formula for gauging how high this critical mass needs to be in concrete cases, but one thing is certain: It will be less than 100 percent.

This insight into the conditions for successful change relieves pressure on the one hand and provides encouragement on the other. It demonstrates that it is worth it to initiate reforms, even if one does not (yet) have everyone on board. The key to success is achieving a critical mass.

Where can I start?

There are many possibilities for change in school and instruction, and our discussion of the previous topic already provides a wealth of material for developing ideas. In the following, we narrow the focus to the issue of how to apply a variety of evidence-based methods, because it is a key factor in making learning visible and thus forms the core of the mindframe "I am a change agent and believe all students can improve."

We would like to begin by pointing out two basic ideas that are particularly relevant at this point of the book but which are a recurrent theme in all the chapters: The mindframe "I am a change agent and believe all students can improve" requires both a constant search for evidence and close cooperation with colleagues. Evidence is necessary because it helps you to determine whether a method achieved the desired effect and whether the changes in the learners that were the goal of your own thinking and actions indeed took place. And because there is often a discrepancy between your own perception of a situation and that of others, it is also critical to discuss your instruction with other teachers. They can help to make your own impact visible, to cast a critical eye on it, and to develop it further in a constructive direction. In this respect, it is your colleagues who provide the impetus for developing your own professionalism and expertise. Four eyes see more than two, one might conclude, or as Martin Buber (1958) would phrase it: A person becomes an I through a You. It is worth noting Chapter 3 on "I collaborate with my peers and my students about conceptions of progress and my impact."

Earlier in this chapter, we argued that learning is dependent on motivation and that we teachers need to have a variety of motivational strategies at our disposal. Start by reflecting on your preferred

Which motivation strategies do I use?

ATTENTION	RELEVANCE	CONFIDENCE	SATISFACTION

strategies on the basis of the ARCS model. To do so, fill out the table above. Discuss your self-assessment with a colleague.

Several studies call attention to the unfortunate fact that teachers spend less time talking about their own instruction than about everything else during a typical school week. That is the reason why many teachers spend many frustrating hours alone trying to decide which motivational strategies to apply during an instructional sequence. This involves didactic creativity, and it is far easier to develop creativity in a team. The next step is, therefore, to get together with a colleague and brainstorm various motivational strategies – first for a concrete lesson and then for an entire instructional sequence. In applying these motivational strategies, make sure to place emphasis on determining what effect they have on the learners, for instance by applying various feedback methods and considering their learning performance during the lesson. Discuss these points with your colleagues and press each other to produce data. What is crucial is not your gut feeling but the realities, and the best way to make these realities visible is through successful learning. Review everything and keep what works best. And take evidence as your touchstone. A good way to do this is by completing the following table, which allows you to keep tabs on the success of the evidence-based motivational strategies you applied in a particular instructional sequence.

Motivational strategies and their effectiveness from the perspective of the learners

ATTENTION		RELEVANCE		CONFIDENCE		SATISFACTION	
	high middle low		high middle low		high middle low		high middle low
	high middle low		high middle low		high middle low		high middle low
	high middle low		high middle low		high middle low		high middle low

It is also possible to draw up similar tables on other instructional principles, illustrating the variety of methods you apply on the one hand and documenting their effectiveness from the perspective of the learners on the other. They may include various means of differentiation to help you make decisions on goals, content, methods, media, space, and time. The table below provides an example you can again complete together with a colleague to prepare for a particular instructional sequence. It allows you to integrate and structure the various achievement levels of the learners – one of the key means of differentiation, if not the most important one of all – including the unistructural, multistructural, relational and extended abtract levels.

A final example we would like to give on account of its effectiveness as presented in this book is deliberate practice. Here as well, it is a good idea to work together with a colleague and develop various strategies, bring them together in a list, and search for evidence to support them. Do not be afraid to use existing worksheets or textbooks for this task. One of the biggest faults of school and instruction, and in particular teacher education, is the practice of leading young teachers to believe that it is best to design everything on their own: There is no need to reinvent the wheel of instruction. There are many good ideas just waiting to be put to use, and there are certainly also many bad ideas that are not even worth trying out. Being able to separate the wheat from the chaff is a hallmark of professionalism. The challenge, therefore, lies in applying existing materials and searching for evidence to determine what works and what does not

Differentiation strategies and their effectiveness from the perspective of the learners

GOALS		CONTENT	METHODS	MEDIA	SPACE
Unistructural level	high middle low	high middle low	high middle low	high middle low	high middle low
Multistructural level	high middle low	high middle low	high middle low	high middle low	high middle low
Relational level	high middle low	high middle low	high middle low	high middle low	high middle low
Extended abstract level	high middle low	high middle low	high middle low	high middle low	high middle low

Exercises and their effectiveness from the perspective of the learner

UNISTRUCT-URAL LEVEL		MULTISTRUCT-URAL LEVEL		RELATIONAL LEVEL		EXTENDED ABSTRACT LEVEL	
Sample task	high middle low	Sample task	high middle low	Sample task	high middle low	Sample task	high middle low

work. Since the initial learning level of the students is also one of the key factors for practice, if not the most important one of all, we have again included the four achievement levels in the table above.

By combining these steps, namely by creating tables and lists for motivation, differentiation, and practice and searching for evidence in support of them, it is possible to establish a basis for learning pathways. These are lesson scripts including suitable methods and media for designing learning arrangements for different instructional goals, thus opening up a variety of options for the learners. They can be adjusted to fit the student's learning level at the start of the lesson and during the further course of the learning process (cf. Hattie, 2014, p. 88). The condition for this is that the teacher must correctly diagnose the students' initial learning level, engage them in an ongoing dialogue, regularly evaluate their instruction, and critique their own approach. The search for evidence is crucial for this process, so it is important to collect feedback, assess the learning process, and conduct other evaluation procedures. The necessary steps for successful learning pathways can be summed up nicely by the acronym DIE in the phrase "Teachers are to DIE for": diagnose (D), intervene (I), and evaluate (E).

CHECKLIST

Reflect on the following points next time you plan a lesson:

- Use a variety of classroom management strategies.
- Try to use preventive strategies to deal with disruptive behavior in your classroom.
- You do not need the full support of your students to initiate changes. Try instead to get a critical mass of learners to believe in your visions.

- Do not reinvent everything. Instead, test what is already available by searching for evidence.

- Develop learning pathways, for instance by applying a variety of motivation, differentiation, and practice strategies. In doing so, do not forget to also include possibilities for making the success of the learning pathways visible.

- Complement your assessment of the methods you choose with assessments from the learners. Demand feedback.

- Talk to colleagues about methods, using evidence to support your views.

EXERCISES

- Go back to the questionnaire for self-reflection at the start of the chapter and complete it again in a different color. Where and, more important, why has your perspective on the statements changed? Discuss your self-assessment with a colleague.

- Design a learning pathway outlining various means of motivation, differentiation, and practice for an instructional sequence. Discuss it with a colleague before teaching the sequence and again after-wards, also including evidence.

- Plan your next lesson, taking account of the students' initial learning level, and include an advance organizer. Discuss your plan and the lesson with a colleague.

I strive for challenge and not merely "doing your best"

> **VIGNETTE**
>
> Every teacher has seen the sparkle in the eyes of a student when learning becomes visible not just in quantifiable terms but also in an emotional sense: The learner accepts the challenge and tackles an assignment that will be difficult. The feeling this learner experiences is plain to see: "It's going to be close. I might not succeed. There's a great danger of failing. But I'm going to try." How much greater is the learner's joy when his or her effort and hard work is followed by success? These are the moments that make teaching worthwhile – like the applause a stage actor receives at the end of a performance.

What is this chapter about?

This vignette illustrates this chapter's main message: Learning needs to be challenging, and it is the main job of the teacher to see to this and at the same time to ensure that the level of challenge is neither too high nor too boring.

When you finish reading this chapter, you should be able to take this message as a basis for explaining:

- how significant the factors "teacher clarity," "goals," and "acceleration" are.
- how to induce a state of flow in lessons.
- what taxonomies of learning goals there are to choose from and how they can be implemented effectively.
- what the Goldilocks principle is and why it is significant for school and instruction.

Which factors from Visible Learning support this mindframe?

It seems practically self-evident that instruction follows goals. Too often, however, teachers do not think about the learning goals when planning lessons (cf. Wernke & Zierer, 2016). Often, they cannot even name their goals after giving the lesson – and neither can the learners: They leave the classroom exactly as they entered it an hour before – but busy work has been accomplished.

Graham Nuthall spent many years listening into the talk among students and with their teachers. What was most apparent from his research was that teachers do not talk to students about learning or thinking; they talk more about paying attention and not annoying others, they talk about the resources the students will need to use, and they talk about activities – how long the activity should take and what will happen if it is not finished on time (Nuthall, 2007). The students talk about the same things: They continually compare how much have they done, how long will it take, do the headings need to be underlined, where did you find that answer, do you have to write it all out? It is clear to Nuthall that students do not become content experts but become experts in classroom procedures that are imprinted upon them lesson after lesson, day after day. The challenge in too many classrooms is about knowing the rules and procedures of the teacher, not the challenge of learning.

Test this out for yourself and ask your students at the end of the class what the goal of the lesson was – choose one lesson you consider to have been successful and another lesson in which you do not think you reached the goal. Do the students talk about the procedures or the content; do they talk about the challenges or having completed the work (regardless of standard), do they talk about the errors, the misconceptions, that which they do not know, the strategies they applied when they were uncertain, the comparisons with others? Certainly, we want students to not say, "This is hard, I cannot or will not do it" but "This is hard, I want to have a try." This is our challenge. This is the essence of the mindframe "I strive for challenge and not merely 'doing your best'."

In the following, we present major factors that relate to developing appropriately challenging learning: "teacher clarity," "goals," and "grade skipping."

Teacher clarity

The factor "teacher clarity" makes it into almost every list of quality standards for instruction: Andreas Helmke (2010), Hilbert Meyer (2013), Jere Brophy (1999), and the MET project (Bill & Melinda Gates Foundation, 2010) all see teacher clarity as one of the linchpins of successful instruction. And so it comes as little surprise that this factor – which is connected with the mindframe "I strive for challenge and not merely 'doing your best'" – achieves an effect size of 0.75 in Visible Learning (see Figure 5.1). What does teacher clarity

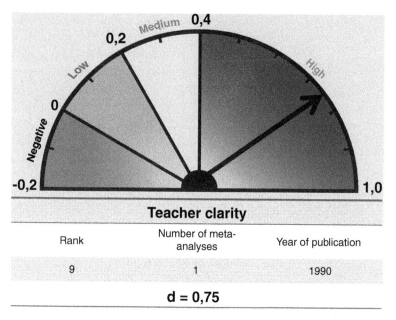

Teacher clarity

Rank	Number of meta-analyses	Year of publication
9	1	1990

d = 0,75

FIGURE 5.1 Teacher clarity

Source: Hattie and Zierer (2017).

involve? The answer lies in an ability to name all of one's planning steps about goals, content, methods, and media and using examples to explain them to students. Teachers who can do this will ultimately also be capable of assigning tasks in such a way that the learners perceive them as a challenge toward a learning goal. But most important is making the goals of the lesson transparent to the students, making the goals appropriately challenging, and providing many ways and opportunities to monitor the progress from where each student begins toward the goals of the lesson.

Goals

The factor "goals" achieves an effect size of 0.50 in Visible Learning (see Figure 5.2). Goals are closely related to several other factors already touched on in this book, particularly aligning with the mindframe "I focus on learning and the language of learning."

In that discussion, we called attention to the fact that learning processes are more successful based on the degree that teachers consider their students' prior knowledge. This includes knowing where students are in their learning, how they think about their learning and

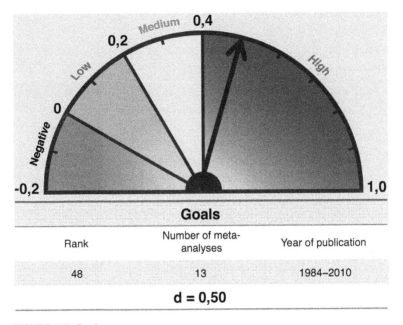

FIGURE 5.2 Goals

Source: Hattie and Zierer (2017).

experiences and what they bring from the home and their culture, and then taking this prior learning as the basis for your teaching and instruction. This implies that it may be necessary to define goals at different levels of difficulty for different students, which is an issue we will discuss later. Another important point in this context is that we are not referring to the goals one typically finds specified in curricula. Curricular goals are often much too distant from the learners – too far from the learning on a specific lesson or day. More concrete instructional goals are needed to meet the specific requirements that students should use to enable them to focus on explicit learning goals.

The most important aspect about goals is that they should specify the level of challenge to be attained in the lesson – in terms of the ideas, relations between ideas, or transfer of knowledge and understanding to new tasks. It is the degree of mastery that needs to be communicated. Mager (1997) adds three further worthwhile criteria (although his third is close to our key attribute of challenging goals):

1. They need to describe the observable behaviors the learners should exhibit by the end of the lesson (e.g., writing down, calculating, reading).

2. They need to name conditions for monitoring the learners' behavior (e.g., how much time is allowed to complete the assignment, which aids are permitted, whether they can work together with other learners).

3. They need to specify standards of evaluation for determining whether and to what extent the learners have achieved the goal (e.g., how many of the tasks need to be completed correctly).

This also illustrates why the advice "do your best" heard so often in pedagogical contexts is not very helpful for the learning process. It is much too vague, too imprecise, and too arbitrary to allow a detailed and compelling analysis. Indeed, most of the studies in the meta-analyses contrast "do your best" with "appropriately challenging" tasks, and this leads to major differences in the quality of learning. If, for example, a runner (Jesse) sets the goal of doing his best on a 10-kilometer course, how is he supposed to evaluate the run? Jesse is better off setting a concrete time as a goal and attempting to achieve it – such as running the 10 kilometers in less than 60 minutes. This goal would be all the more powerful if it related to Jesse's personal best time. Hence, we see the goal becomes an appropriately challenging task. In addition, it alludes to one of the key points of successful goals: It is not enough for teachers to be clear about the goals of their instruction. As important as this is, it is only the first step. The second step involves seeing to it that this clarity is also understood by the learners by reaching an understanding with them as to how the learning should proceed and making the criteria for successful learning to be visible.

Rather than saying "do your best," consider the value of "personal bests." At least "personal bests" have a sense of accomplishment to reference our current learning. What have we already understood, and can we learn more or better than that? Andrew Martin (2012) has shown that "personal bests" positively predict students' aspirations, class participation, enjoyment of school, perseverance and engagement at school tasks, and achievement and effort on tests. The major value of "personal bests" is that they make the goals "owned" by the students, make it clear to them what they need to strive for to outperform a previous best, help direct attention and effort toward the goal-relevant tasks, create an internal pressure to perform while arousing energy and effort, and thus can energize students to persevere and stay on task (often despite failure) to reach the "personal bests." "Personal bests" can relate to each of Mager's criteria:

showing more or better workings, checking and revising work, trying more questions, working collaboratively with others, using time better, seeking advice about the standards of evaluation of success, performing better on assignments (see also Martin, 2012).

Grade skipping (acceleration)

Grade skipping or acceleration is a measure based on the same assumption as holding back or retention: helping the learner by making a structural adjustment to the learning speed. In terms of their effects and frequency, however, these factors could not be more different. Whereas students are held back more often, they are very few who are allowed to skip a grade, and whereas retention has negative effects (−.13), acceleration leads to positive effects (.68) (see Figure 5.3). Why is skipping grades so successful? What happens here that fails to happen when a child is held back? The meta-analyses included in Visible Learning suggest that it is not the structural measure of retention as such but primarily what transpires in the ensuing interactions: Learners who have been held back tend to stagnate in their learning, because they often spend the

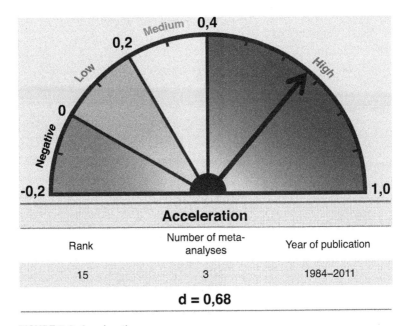

Rank	Number of meta-analyses	Year of publication
15	3	1984–2011

d = 0,68

FIGURE 5.3 Acceleration

Source: Hattie and Zierer (2017).

year sitting in a similar classroom, doing similar work, with similar interactions. Only in rare cases do they (or their teachers) actually tackle the problems that led to their retention and take their failure in the learning process as an opportunity. Only in rare cases are in-depth discussions with all involved held and a detailed and differentiated plan for remedial study drawn up. As a consequence, students repeating a grade usually do not learn anything new but are simply bored, get the powerful message that they are not learners, and make the same mistakes they made the previous year. Acceleration leads to different interactions: Learners who skip a grade receive tasks that are more appropriately challenging to their achievement level than the ones they received before. The instruction is now adjusted to fit the learner's sense of challenge.

The basic principle of acceleration – challenging learning – can be achieved by methods other than grade skipping, such as mastery learning (advance when the standard of learning achieved), self-paced instructions, compacting the curriculum, throwing a lot of surface knowledge out of the curricula, telescoping (completing more quickly so as to move to more challenging work), use of online courses to help speed up learning, advanced placement, or early graduation. It is pitching the learning with transparent and challenging goals. The alternative is boredom, busy work, and turning students off learning as a worthwhile task.

Hence, the factors "teacher clarity," "goals," and "acceleration" indicate that successful instruction always leads to challenges for the learners. The most important ingredients for the learners are clarity and appropriate challenge about the goals they are expected to achieve, a resulting understanding about the learning path, and an idea about what makes successful learning visible. Methods that enable all of this are what set the challenge.

Flow and its significance for learning

There have been many studies on the importance of challenges for learning, but the one that stands out is the research on flow conducted by Mihály Csíkszentmihályi (2008). He succeeded in showing that when a learner is deeply involved in the task, and in the zone, they can then experience the deepest and most lasting happiness. When in the zone, they have a sense of personal control over the activity, they seek and interpret immediate feedback, and they feel that they have the potential to achieve success, especially by

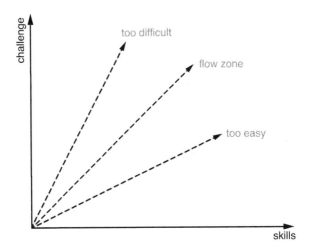

FIGURE 5.4 Flow and its significance for learning

Source: Hattie and Zierer (2017).

investing effort and skill. Flow is more likely to occur when the student knows the goals and his or her progress to the goals (this adds direction and source to the task), when there are opportunities for clear and immediate feedback (as this helps work through changing demands and allows adjustment to performance), and where there is a balance between the perceived challenges of the task and one's own perceived skills. There must be a level of confidence that the student can attain the goals. This balance between perceived abilities and goal demands is often illustrated in the following graph (see Figure 5.4).

The greater the clarity and confidence to attain a challenging goal, the more the learner becomes invested in the flow of learning to attain these goals. The challenge, however, cannot be too high or too low. If it is too high, this can lead to anxiety, not investing effort (why bother if the chances of success are low), and a sense of failure. Too low can lead to boredom. The same applies to the teacher in setting appropriately challenging goals to work with students to activate their learning. It is plain to see that the factors "goals," "personal bests," and "motivation" are important for achieving a state of flow, because taking them into account is the basic requirement for achieving a balance between abilities and demands.

Taxonomies of learning goals: an important step toward Visible Learning and successful teaching

It seems an obvious question to ask: What exactly do teachers who have the mindframe "I strive for challenge and not merely 'doing your best'" do differently? Research in connection with taxonomies of learning goals has shown that there are observable differences in teacher behavior in regard to what challenging compared to non-challenging teachers do and think.

The starting point for this research was the development of models like the SOLO taxonomy ("structure of observed learning outcomes") developed by John Biggs and Kevin Collis (1982). This taxonomy consists of five levels ranging from incompetence to expertise:

- prestructural level: no knowledge
- unistructural level: knowledge of one relevant aspect
- multistructural level: knowledge of several relevant independent aspects
- relational level: knowledge of several integrated aspects
- extended abstract level: knowledge generalized to new domains.

To make it simple: no idea, one idea, many ideas, relate ideas, and extend ideas. While the second and third levels cover surface understanding, the fourth and fifth levels refer to deeper understanding. This taxonomy has been used in classroom observations to determine how the work assigned by experienced teachers differs from that assigned by expert teachers – with teachers defined as expert if they passed the US National Board for Professional Teaching Standards and experienced those teachers who sat but did not pass. The results are presented in Figure 5.5 (cf. Hattie, 2014, p. 33).

Thus, while most of the work assigned by experienced teachers aims at the level of surface understanding, that assigned by expert teachers aims primarily at the level of deep understanding. Note, what is important is the proportions of surface and deep, not one or the other. The key question here is how this difference comes about. Contrary to what one might suspect, it is not that expert teachers constantly assign loads of work aimed at deep understanding. This would be too much to ask of any teacher, and it ignores the fact that surface understanding is the basis for deep understanding. Rather,

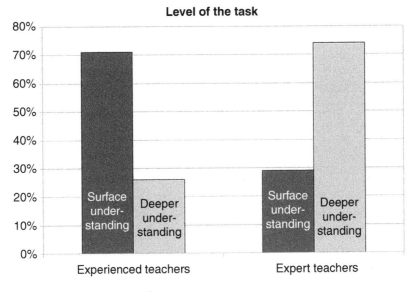

Level of the task

FIGURE 5.5 Level of the task

the difference stems from the observation that experienced teachers remain too long at the level of surface understanding and so miss the moment at which it would be prudent to penetrate into the challenge of deep understanding, of asking students to make relations between ideas and extend these ideas (particularly to new contexts). This approach demands more of the learners by presenting them with challenges in the learning process.

Another example of not challenging students is that students often know 50 percent of what they are supposed to learn in school and instruction before the lesson starts (cf. Nuthall, 2007). This eventuates mainly because teachers do not set appropriately challenging goals but simply run through a set routine, provide lots of monologue, assign busy work, and thus do not challenge the students.

This brings us to our vignette from Chapter 10: Victoria learned the number 1 in her first week as a first grader, the number 2 in her second week, the number 3 in her third week, and so on. At the end of the first week, she asked why she had to learn things she already learned in preschool. And what made things even worse was that she had to color the numbers as she learned them – an activity she had enjoyed in preschool but was not challenged by now. What a way to turn students off of the fun of learning.

The Goldilocks principle

The ideas presented so far in this chapter may be elucidated further by means of a concept known in the literature as the Goldilocks principle after the popular children's story "Goldilocks and the Three Bears": A girl named Goldilocks enters a house owned by three bears. Each of the three bears has its own preference in regard to eating, sitting, and sleeping. After testing the food, chairs, and beds of all three bears one after the other, the girl comes to the following conclusion: The first bear's food is too hot, its chair is too big, and its bed is too hard; the second bear's food is too cold, its chair is too small, and its bed is too soft; but the third bear's food, chair, and bed are just right.

The main message of the story is that there is always a "just right" between extremes that fits best under particular conditions. This effect has been applied to various disciplines. In medicine, for example, the dosage of a drug can be too high or too low, and in communication studies it has been shown that a company can offer too many or too few opportunities for discussion between employees. In many contexts, it is ultimately the golden mean or the right measure that decides over success or failure – a notion that goes all the way back to Aristotle (Moral behavior is between two extremes – at one end is excess, at the other is deficiency. Find a moderate position between those two extremes, and you will be acting morally.).

If we apply this principle to school and instruction, we arrive at an insight that will be pointed out in Chapter 10, "I focus on learning and the language of learning," that is absolutely essential for the mindframe "I strive for challenge and not merely 'doing your best'." It is not very helpful to confront a learner who is working at the SOLO levels of learning an idea or ideas with more difficult tasks at the level of transfer, just as it makes little sense to confront a learner working at the level of problem solving with easier surface tasks. We need to get our challenges "just right." The point is we need to adjust the level of difficulty just above the learner's current achievement level. If the teacher succeeds in doing this, the learners will be presented with a challenge and the stage will be set for the optimal learning success. It goes without saying that the teacher needs to have the competence and the mindframe necessary to implement the Goldilocks principle. What this means above all is the effort to do justice to each and every learner and the ability to formulate and communicate differentiated but challenging goals.

A recent study, however, moves the Goldilocks principle from "not too hard, not too easy" to "not too hard, not too boring." Lomas et al. (2017) offered video game players a choice of difficulty or random assigning difficulty. When the difficulty was randomly assigned, easier games were more motivating but when players had a choice, moderately difficult games were most motivating. The adage thus is now changed to be "not too hard, not too boring." Students will engage in challenging tasks, even very high levels of challenge if the tasks are interesting and seen as worthwhile and certainly not boring. Hence, we need to engage the students in more challenging tasks, by devising optimal lessons, providing appropriate problems and tasks, and making goals more transparent so students focus on the challenging processes and know when they have succeeded. As we noted earlier, using the notion of "personal bests" could be powerful to have students engage in more challenging tasks, having high commitment to attaining these "personal bests."

Where can I start?

The following two areas are a good place to start working on developing the mindframe "I strive for challenge and not merely 'doing your best'." First, it is worth it to cast a critical eye on the tasks you aim to assign in class – if possible, together with colleagues. The important thing to consider is the SOLO achievement level that is targeted. If too many of the tasks are aimed at a particular level, spend some time preparing questions or tasks aimed at the next levels up the taxonomy. Second, it is worth it to reflect critically on how your goals are formulated. Start by comparing the two examples below and discussing their usefulness with a colleague.

Example 1

Learners should be able to write the salutation for a business letter.

Example 2

Learners should be able to write an appropriate salutation for at least eight of ten business letters provided to them.

For further reflection on goal formulation, consider our discussion of Mager's assertion that effective instructional goals need to take account of the learners' observable behavior, the conditions for monitoring their behavior, and their (and your) standards for evaluation. What conclusions can you draw from these criteria? How might the previous examples be optimized, also in regard to the unistructural, multistructural, relational and extended abstract levels? These two factors form the basis of what is called the 1+ strategy in Visible Learning: raising the standards bit by bit with each new task and thus challenging the learners again and again to perform above the best of their current abilities.

Computer games like Angry Birds are a good illustration of this idea, because they are structured precisely according to this principle: The game knows your prior achievement (your last score or level). It then sets a more challenging level on the principles of making the challenge not too hard, not too boring. Then there is much opportunity for deliberate practice by seeking help, trialing again, asking friends, searching for tips, and all the time gaining feedback about how close to the new personal best level. You know you have succeeded when the next level is reached. And unlike many teachers, the message then is not "hand in the work, you have finished" but the rising to the next level of challenge – and so the flow and love of learning continues. This analogy might seem somewhat simplistic, but it carries a message that is also important for teachers: If we want learners to make progress, we need to take into account their initial learning level and adjust the tasks we assign them to match it with appropriately more challenging tasks – and in such a way that the learners are capable of completing them – not too hard and not too boring.

Too often, teachers forget the "Angry Birds" message – they assign the same tasks to all students regardless of their different prior achievements. They do not tell students what success looks like (until after completion of the task), and the success so often is complete the task, hand it in, and success is really when the work is over for the day. For some this might be challenging, but it is not motivating or engaging and is unlikely to lead students to wanting to invest in further challenging learning.

CHECKLIST

Consider the following points next time you plan a lesson:

- Ensure goal clarity for your students by making your goals clear to yourself.
- Try to reach an understanding with your learners in regard to your goals.

- Make it clear what learning success involves and how it should be made visible.
- Take out the analysis of your students' initial learning level you made in the last chapter and use it as a basis for formulating goals at different achievement levels.
- Make sure the tasks you assign in class represent different levels.
- Use a taxonomy of learning goals.
- Set differentiated goals that ensure a balance between difficulty level and achievement level.
- Integrate a phase into your lesson in which you can compare your assessment of the level of the goals and tasks with that of your students.
- When formulating your goals, try to make sure they describe observable behavior, name conditions for monitoring this behavior, and include standards for evaluation.
- Double-check to make sure your goals are clear and adjusted to the learners.

EXERCISES

- Go back to the questionnaire for self-reflection at the start of the chapter and complete it again in another color. Where and, more important, why has your perspective on the statements changed? Discuss your self-assessment with a colleague.
- Formulate goals at the level of reproduction, reorganization, transfer, unistructural, multistructural, relational and extended abstract levels for your next lesson. Create tasks to complete during class and as homework. Discuss the goals and the tasks with a colleague.
- Carry out your lesson plan and discuss the learning tasks at different levels with your students. Take this feedback as an opportunity to reconsider your goal formulations and learning tasks in another discussion with a colleague.
- Ask your students to write down the goal of the lesson and compare their responses with your lesson plan. Take this feedback as an opportunity to engage your students and a colleague in a dialogue.

6

I give and help students understand feedback and I interpret and act on feedback given to me

---

QUESTIONNAIRE FOR SELF-REFLECTION

Assess yourself by rating your agreement with the following statements: 1 = strongly disagree, 5 = strongly agree

I am very good at . . .

obtaining feedback from my students.

using the feedback from my students to improve my teaching.

I know perfectly well . . .

that I need to act on the feedback from my students.

how to give and help students understand feedback.

My goal is always to . . .

obtain feedback from my students.

reflect on the feedback from my students.

I am thoroughly convinced . . .

that regular feedback strategies need to be integrated into my lessons.

that I should use my students' opinions as feedback for me.

VIGNETTE

What teacher is not familiar with moments like the following? You have spent a lot of time and effort planning a lesson and go into the classroom highly motivated and well prepared, but it does not go off as planned: The introduction fails to produce the intended reaction, the learners are restless, and in the end, you have the feeling of not having taught them anything at all. You leave the classroom dissatisfied and without really knowing what happened. Although you would rather start from scratch with a new lesson plan the next day, you decide to ask the learners what they thought of the lesson. Much to your surprise, you discover that you were mistaken: The learners tell you they found the lesson interesting and that they had to make a lot of effort to achieve the goal. A pop quiz also produces convincing results. More than satisfied with this state of affairs, you set off to tackle the next challenges together with the students.

What is this chapter about?

This vignette illustrates this chapter's main message: Teachers cannot answer the question of whether learning and teaching is successful on their own. They need to ask the learners what they think, because they provide crucial input. The most powerful form of feedback is from the students to the teachers about their impact on the students. Learning and teaching are dialogic processes. Successful teachers are thus capable both of giving students feedback on their learning processes and of demanding and interpreting feedback from students on their own teaching processes.

When you finish reading this chapter, you should be able to take this message as a basis for explaining:

- how significant the factors "questioning," "metacognitive strategies," "study skills," and "classroom discussion" are.
- what makes successful feedback.
- what it means to give comprehensive feedback.
- what it means to obtain meaningful feedback from the learners.

- what misunderstood feedback (praise, peers, etc.) can involve.
- what the basic principles of feedback in class are.

Which factors from Visible Learning support this mindframe?

One of the main messages of Visible Learning is the significance of feedback for the learning process. Learners need the teacher's feedback, but teachers also need the learner's feedback. Again, the key questions are the following: Did the lesson achieve the success criteria? Did the learners understand the content? Did the students make connections to prior learning and among the content leading to deeper understanding? Were the methods the teacher applied successful? Did the students get enjoyment out of knowing they were learning? All these questions can ultimately be answered only by the learners, and it is, therefore, the teacher's job to listen and seek feedback from the learners about his or her own impact.

Finding the answers does not necessarily involve asking the students straight out what they thought of your lesson, although this is certainly a possibility. Rather, it involves drawing on all forms of feedback in the classroom, or even searching actively for all possible forms of information on the success or failure of learning processes, and reflecting on their relation to your own teaching. Consider the following illustration in Figure 6.1.

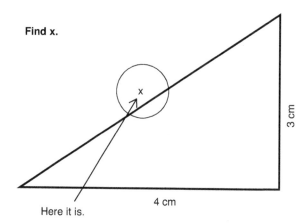

FIGURE 6.1 Find x

Source: Hattie and Zierer (2017).

The mistake the learner made here should be immediately apparent to any math teacher. The answer "Here it is" does not solve the problem. Rather, solving it needs to involve applying the Pythagorean theorem: $x = 5$ cm. However, simply marking the answer as mathematically incorrect and leaving it at that would be a waste of a good opportunity, because the main message of this mistake lies elsewhere and has more to do with the teacher than with the learner: The teacher failed in conveying the point of the problem or making the task clear. In other words, the teacher failed to *make learning visible* to the learner.

This example emphasizes the importance of seeing oneself as an evaluator – both of the student's learning process and of one's own teaching process. The key to doing so is to give and demand feedback. In general, teachers agree that feedback is important in the classroom, and they, therefore, include a lot of feedback in their lessons. However, giving and demanding successful feedback is not such a simple matter. It is as important to be concerned with how feedback is received as much as how it is given, and the feedback we receive as teachers is often more powerful than feedback students receive – as we demonstrate in the following.

A good place to start is by looking at Visible Learning: It includes several factors that further emphasize the significance of the mindframe "I give and help students understand feedback and I interpret and act on feedback given to me." These factors are "questioning," "metacognitive strategies," "study skills," and classroom discussion.

Questioning

The factor "questioning" achieves a correspondingly high effect size of 0.48 in Visible Learning (see Figure 6.2). The major issue in most of the questioning research relates to asking "higher order" or "deeper question." This is because 90 percent of most questions are about the facts, the surface level of learning, and teachers ask lots of questions (some argue 150+ a day). It is asking the higher cognitive questions that allow for relating ideas, creating connections with prior knowledge, and creating discussions so that the teacher can "hear" the impact of teaching. Structuring class sessions to entice, teach, and listen to student questioning of each other also is powerful.

The teacher can optimize the power of questions by making them either at the current level of student learning – plus one. That is, if the student is at the surface level of learning then ask surface questions but also a smaller percentage of deeper questions to help move

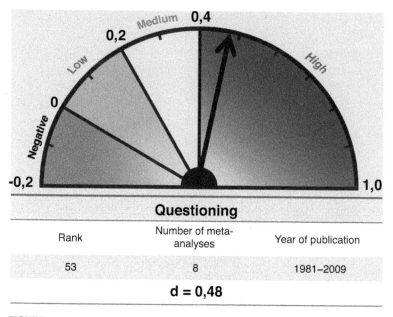

Questioning

Rank	Number of meta-analyses	Year of publication
53	8	1981–2009

d = 0,48

FIGURE 6.2 Questioning

Source: Hattie and Zierer (2017).

to consolidate where they are and to move them plus one to the next phase. If they are at the deeper level, then ask transfer questions to help apply to a new task.

Questions posed by the learners can indicate to the teacher where the learners need support, what is not yet clear to them, what interests them, and where to go next. Providing scope for these questions, paying attention to them, and taking them up in class are hallmarks of successful teachers.

Metacognitive strategies

"Metacognition" is a term for thinking about one's own thought processes. The associated factor "metacognitive strategies" achieves an effect size of 0.69 in Visible Learning, placing it near the top ten (see Figure 6.3). Much more important than this ranking, however, is the message from research in this area: Questioning one's own learning, attempting to make learning visible for oneself, and using mistakes to reflect on the structure and coherence of one's own action – all of this is highly influential for learning, because it fosters dialogue

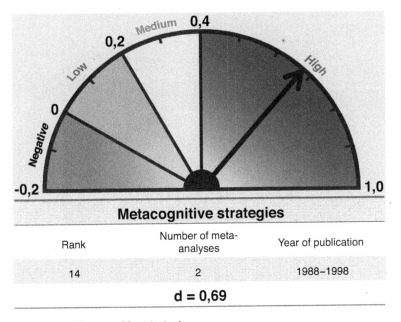

Metacognitive strategies

Rank	Number of meta-analyses	Year of publication
14	2	1988–1998

d = 0,69

FIGURE 6.3 Metacognitive strategies

Source: Hattie and Zierer (2017).

between learners and teachers. The attempt to think about thinking leads to a critical examination of learning and teaching, makes that which one understands and does not yet understand visible, and thus provides indications on how to plan the next lesson. Students who are able to self-regulate in these ways are very good at seeking and using feedback. A major aim, therefore, is to teach students these skills of help seeking and interpreting feedback so it is a necessary part of how they learn.

Study skills

Another factor with a comparable influence on the learning process is "study skills." It has an effect size of 0.63 in Visible Learning (see Figure 6.4). Skills that help learners to take notes, review and assimilate material in a meaningful way, prepare summaries, regulate their own motivation, set goals for themselves, or structure and control learning processes lead to lasting improvements in performance, both in the domain of surface understanding and in that of deep understanding. In our more recent synthesis relating to "how we learn," a

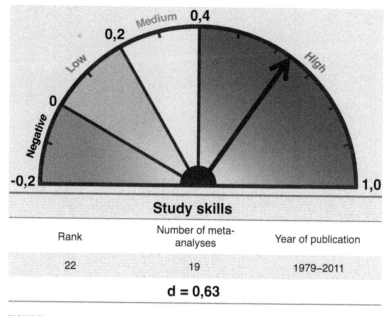

Study skills

Rank	Number of meta-analyses	Year of publication
22	19	1979–2011

d = 0,63

FIGURE 6.4 Study skills

Source: Hattie and Zierer (2017).

much more strategic role is found in the use of learning strategies. The same strategies can work differently when the task is about the surface learning compared with when it is about the deep or transfer of learning, and they can differ when a student is beginning to acquire compared with consolidating the intentions of the lesson. Thus, the teacher needs to seek feedback about where the student is in the learning cycle (surface, deep, transfer) and whether first being exposed or aiming to consolidate the learning (see Hattie & Donoghue, 2016).

We could easily describe other factors to illustrate the main message of this chapter here – such as "reciprocal teaching" (0.74), "teaching strategies" (0.62), or "self-verbalization and self-questioning" (0.64). They are all directly related to the factors discussed earlier. However, one factor we have dealt with only implicitly so far stands out above all the others and merits explicit treatment here: feedback. It is the key factor for highlighting the significance of the mindframe "I give and help students understand feedback and I interpret and act on feedback given to me" and for demonstrating that the structure of successful instruction is fundamentally dialogic.

Know thy impact: feedback as the key to successful instruction

"Feedback" is among the most thoroughly researched methods of all and is one of the most powerful influences on learning performance: Visible Learning cites 25 meta-analyses with an average effect size of 0.75 in the last 30 years alone. The major issue, however, is that the same feedback can be powerful or harmful, as the variance of the impact of feedback is among the highest of all education influences.

This is where the studies conducted within the context of Visible Learning (see also Hattie & Timperley, 2007) assist. They provide a means of determining the quality of different feedback questions and different types of feedback and aim to understand why and how feedback can be so variable. They outlined three major feedback questions: Where am I going? How am I going? and Where to next? They also made a basic distinction between four levels of feedback that can be administered to achieve various effects, as shown in the table below.

Each of the three feedback questions can be addressed at each of these levels. While many teachers tend to define and use feedback more in terms of "How am I going?" and "Where am I going?" students are more adamant that feedback is powerful when it addresses "Where to next?" Students overwhelmingly prefer feedback that addresses the third question "Where to next?" whereas nearly all the feedback provided is about the first two questions. Yes, the "Where to next" feedback can be (and probably should be) based on feedback relating to "Where am I going?", and "How am I going?", but the message is clear – ensure that there is always "Where to next?" feedback.

SELF-LEVEL	TASK LEVEL	PROCESS LEVEL	SELF-REGULATION LEVEL
Personal evaluations and effect (usually positive) on the learner	How well tasks are understood/ performed	The process needed to understand/ perform tasks	Self-monitoring, directing, and regulating of actions

Person-based feedback: the self

The first level is the self. It includes all feedback aimed at the individual receiving the feedback, such as praise as well as criticism of all kinds: "That was fantastic," "You're great," "You're a hard-working student," or "Good job!" The effects of this type of feedback on learning are small to zero. This is because feedback at the self-level does not include any information on the learning process but is focused almost entirely on personality traits. It can even lead to negative effects in some cases, because learners register these forms of feedback as exactly what they are: an assessment of their own person. Excessive praise can lead to a reduction in willingness to try, because learners tend to avoid putting a positive image of themselves on the line too often. Similarly, criticism can lead to a negative self-concept, because it is not directed to the learning material and any mistakes the learner may have made but to the learner's personality.

The biggest problem with praise is that it can interfere with the message about the work. Like most of us, students are more likely to recall the praise and reduce or ignore the information about the task. Try giving feedback about the work with and without praise – and then ask students (say a day later so it is not just pure memory effects) what they recall about the feedback you gave them yesterday – more often than not they recall the praise and not the information about the task. Praise can overpower useful feedback.

Feedback at the self-level is especially problematic for learners who are already intrinsically motivated, because the feedback then works as a type of extrinsic motivation. This can lead in the worst case to a reduction in intrinsic motivation and a corresponding increase in extrinsic motivation – and the last thing a teacher wants is an extrinsically motivated learner, because it is psychologically undesirable. Learners with high intrinsic motivation and low extrinsic motivation learn more effectively and retain and apply more of what they have learned. They are inspired by the love of learning.

We are certainly NOT saying that you should not praise or give feedback about the self. We are saying do not mix praise with feedback about the work, as praise acts as a diluter.

One area in which feedback aimed at the self can be useful is building teacher – student relationships, where it actually can have a positive effect. However, there are many effective means of creating an atmosphere of security, confidence, and trust between the teacher and the student, which we will treat in more detail in our discussion of the mindframe "I build relationships and trust so that learning can occur in a place where it is safe to make mistakes and learn from others." All in all, there is general agreement among researchers that feedback directed at the self-level should be given only in well-measured and carefully considered doses – and not mixed with feedback about the task, processes, or self-regulation. The principle of "less is more" is often the best guide for self-feedback.

Performance-based feedback: task, process, and self-regulation

Unlike feedback at the self-level, which we termed person-based feedback, the task, process, and self-regulation levels all have to do with the learner's performance. Feedback at these levels is always more effective, but to varying degrees, as a closer look shows.

Feedback at the task level involves providing the learners information about the product of their learning. For example, the teacher can assign a task with problems the learners must solve to reach the learning goal. The teacher corrects the task and marks the answers as correct or incorrect. In this way, the learners see clearly *what they can and cannot do.*

Feedback at the process level involves providing the learners information about the process they used to complete the learning task. For example, the teacher can inspect the task for evidence of how the learners completed them. The task might look like they were completed quickly, or there may be signs of sloppiness or a lot of careless mistakes, to name just a few examples. In this case, the learners receive information about *how they worked.* They can also receive feedback identifying errors and suggestions for addressing them and about different methods they might use to tackle the tasks, and they can be asked to make different kinds of connections between parts of the task.

Feedback at the self-regulation level involves providing the learners information about the mechanisms they apply to regulate their learning. For example, the teacher can report back to the learners that they want to invest more effort into various parts, ask them to consider whether they think this part is effective and invite them to revisit, invite the student to think more about the correctness of a section and what they could do better, and in general to encourage the student to make their own judgments, directions, and improvements (and check these with the teacher). The student is more the agent of improvement considering your feedback. This type of feedback makes it clear to the learners *how they self-regulated the product and process of their learning.*

Bringing the levels of feedback together

Imagine another teacher is sitting in on one of your lessons, and afterwards you sit down to discuss how the lesson went. What kind of feedback would you like to receive most if you had to choose: Would you choose feedback at the task level that shows you what you did right and what you did wrong *in the lesson*? Would you choose feedback at the process level that focuses on your planning process *before the lesson* and how you implemented this plan? Or would you choose feedback at the self-regulation level that invites you to talk with your colleague about how you thought the lesson had an impact on students and what you could do to make it more effective in *the next lesson*?

It is also worth inviting a colleague to observe your lesson and monitor the various forms of feedback you give to students. We have done this both with verbal feedback in the class and written feedback on tasks. We have conducted a survey on the nature of feedback (written and verbal) that hundreds of teachers provide. The outcome is always the same: The clear majority of teachers prefer to give and receive feedback at the self-regulation level, whereas only very few would ask for or give feedback at the task or process level. This shows that feedback at the self-regulation level has a special status for learners – after all, you are the learner in this fictitious example. If one considers the feedback that is given daily in classrooms with this point in mind, one obtains the following picture, as shown in the table below.

Hence, the kind of feedback learners want and need most is the kind they receive least often, and the kind they regard as the least important is the kind they receive most often. While there is nothing wrong with feedback at the task level, it is hard to imagine that the task is so dominant in so many of these classrooms. How much more

	HATTIE & MASTERS (2011)	VAN DEN BERGH, ROS, & BEIJAARD (2010)	GAN (2011)
Level	18 high school classes	32 middle school teachers	235 peers
Task	59%	51%	70%
Process	25%	42%	25%
Self-regulation	2%	2%	1%
Self	14%	5%	4%

could teachers achieve just by putting more thought into the levels of feedback they give to their students?

Finally, what also becomes clear in this connection is that successful feedback is not a matter of quantity but of quality: What good does it do the learner to hear yet again that he or she has made the same mistake if one does not also give him or her concrete information on why he or she keeps making it and how he or she can avoid making it in the future? In other words, providing more feedback at the task level does not result in any far-reaching effects. Only if it is combined with feedback at the process and self-regulation level will it have a substantial impact: We need to think of the +1 notion: Provide feedback at the level the student is currently working at but sprinkle it with feedback at the next level to entice them to move upward in their learning (see Figure 6.5).

This movement upward will not happen automatically. What good does it do for the learner to hear not just five but ten times which mistake he or she has made? This will not lead to a greater learning. They want to move forward in their learning to then understand the processes and strategies of learning and ultimately to have some regulation over their own learning.

We do not wish to create the impression that one feedback level is better than another. The message we are trying to convey here is rather that the various feedback levels are connected and interact with each other. The trick is thus not to give feedback at the right level but to give feedback at the appropriate level but with a focus on moving upward through the levels with the learning of the student.

These considerations reveal three key insights for successful feedback: First, feedback is most powerful when given at or just

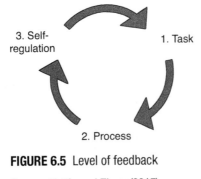

FIGURE 6.5 Level of feedback

Source: Hattie and Zierer (2017).

above the level the student is working (task process, self-regulation). Second, each of the levels can be reductive if applied exclusively, because the result will be insufficient information and monotony, and we do not want the student to stand still. Third, teachers can enhance the effectiveness of all the levels by providing feedback about "where to next."

Novice – advanced learner – expert: the role of achievement level

Our discussion of feedback levels raises the question as to whether the balance between them is dependent on the achievement level of the learners. Consider the following example.

Picture a learner who is completely new to a field and can, therefore, claim the status of novice. This learner does not yet have any insight into any subject matter, is not yet capable of establishing any contextual relationships, and does not yet comprehend the basic elements of the field in question. Take, for example, a first grader who is learning how to count to 20: What level of feedback is needed? Now, compare the feedback you would give this learner with the feedback you would give an expert on a topic in her field. She is familiar with her area of expertise, knows where the pitfalls lie, and has profound insight into the field. Take, for example, Tiger Woods, Roger Federer, or Lady Gaga: Which level of feedback do they need in matters of golf, tennis, or music? It should be clear that a novice requires a different focus of feedback than an expert. Whereas the novice needs first to know what he or she is doing wrong and thus requires feedback at the task level, the expert will benefit more from feedback at the self-regulation level. The learner from the previous example might not know that $3 + 6 = 8$ is incorrect – and who could blame her? An expert, on the other hand, generally knows full well what he is doing wrong – Tiger Woods knows that the ball he hit landed in the rough, Roger Federer knows that his serve is going out of bounds, and Lady Gaga knows that the music is off key. But we all need expert help to understand these mistakes and regulate our learning processes better.

This does not mean we should always give the bright students feedback at the self-regulation level, and not-so-bright students get feedback at the task level. Every student starts many lessons as a novice and thus can start with feedback at the task level, and all students can be helped by the feedback to move through task to process to self-regulation. Thus, applying the optimal form of feedback depending on where the student is in the learning cycle helps explain why there is so much variability in the power of feedback. The same feedback may work or not work depending on where the student is in their learning; however, in nearly all cases ensuring that there is, at least, some "Where to next?" feedback helps the impact of the feedback.

Past – present – future: three perspectives of feedback

In addition to distinguishing between four levels of feedback, Visible Learning (see also Hattie & Timperley, 2007) also argues that each of these levels can be seen from three different perspectives: "feed up," "feed back," and "feed forward." This takes us into a more profound dimension of feedback, demonstrating the complexity of a factor that seems so straightforward at first glance. What do these three perspectives involve concretely?

"Feed up" is feedback that compares the learner's current state with the desired target state. It is thus focused on the present and may be defined as feedback on the present. "Feed back" is feedback that compares the learner's current state with a previous state. It is thus focused on the past and may be defined as feedback on the past. And finally, "feed forward" is feedback that illustrates the desired target state based on the learner's current state. It is, therefore, directed to the future and may defined as feedback on the future (this is more the "Where to next?" feedback, preferred by students).

In giving feedback on the results of an achievement test, for example, the teacher can give the learners three types of task-level feedback: *first*, feedback on the problems they solved correctly and incorrectly, thus describing their current state in comparison to the desired target state ("feed up"); *second*, feedback on how their achievement level has changed in comparison to the last achievement test, where they have improved, and where they have not improved, thus describing their current state in comparison to their previous current state ("feed back"); and *third*, feedback on the tasks they need to complete in the future and the target state this should lead them to ("feed forward").

Hence, successful feedback may be focused on a past, present, or future perspective. All three are connected and together make up an integrated whole: Feedback on the present is based on feedback

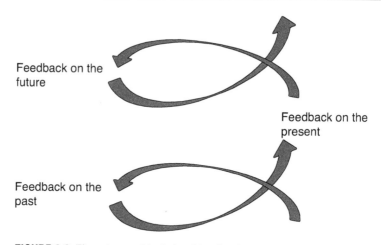

Feedback on the future

Feedback on the present

Feedback on the past

FIGURE 6.6 Three types of task-level feedback

Source: Hattie and Zierer (2017).

on the past and is itself a precursor of feedback on the future (see Figure 6.6).

As we noted earlier, the question most students prefer to be answered by the feedback is "Where to next," which is more powerful when it itself is based on Where am I going? and How am I going? As many researchers have noted, this points to a major role of feedback – to close the gap between where the student starts and where they are optimally ending in the sequence of lessons.

A call for comprehensive feedback: the feedback matrix

Visible Learning emphasizes again and again that successful feedback should be as comprehensive as possible, but what does comprehensive feedback involve? Which areas does the teacher need to concentrate on? How can the teacher combine the levels of feedback with the perspectives of feedback? Although one of the greatest achievements of the Visible Learning project is to have drawn attention back to feedback, several things remain unclear in practice. In the following, we therefore attempt to integrate the levels and perspectives of feedback into a feedback matrix including sample questions.

	LEVELS OF FEEDBACK		
	TASK	PROCESS	SELF-REGULATION
Past ("feed back")	What progress has the learner made on goals and content?	What progress has the learner made on task completion? Is there evidence of improvement?	What progress has the learner made on self-regulation strategies?
Present ("feed up")	What goals did the learner reach? What content did the learner understand?	How did the learner complete the task? Is there evidence of how the learner worked?	What self-regulation strategies did the learner successfully apply?
Future ("feed forward")	What goals should be set next? What content should be learned next?	What tips on task completion should the learner be given next?	What self-regulation strategies should the learner apply next?

Perspectives of feedback (vertical label spanning the left of the rows)

Give and take: on the dialogic structure of feedback

Discussions on feedback are regularly dominated by the notion that feedback should be directed from the teacher to the learner. The teacher is said to be responsible for giving the students detailed and comprehensive feedback on their learning as often as possible. As important as this is, it is but one of many forms of feedback – and if overdone, it can overload the students and degenerate into a pointless exercise. Never-ending comments on students' learning progress that interest only teachers and administrators may serve as an admittedly exaggerated example of where an overemphasis on teacher feedback to students can lead.

It was precisely this insight that led us to take the long-standing discussion on the influence of feedback on learning in a new direction: Teacher-to-student feedback may be important, but learner-to-teacher feedback is just as or even more important. After all, the teacher cannot answer the questions of whether the students achieved the goals, whether they understood the content, whether the methods were useful, or whether the media were helpful. These

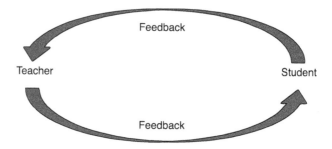

FIGURE 6.7 Dialogic structure of feedback

Source: Hattie and Zierer (2017).

are questions only the learners can answer. The teacher's role is to elicit, listen, and then react. How often do teachers leave the classroom satisfied because everything seems to have gone as planned, whereas the students realize afterwards that they only performed the roles the teacher asked of them to avoid being penalized, not to learn, and were essentially bored by the lesson? Systems theory has a name for this strategy: gaming the system. The only way to overcome this difference between self-assessment and external assessment is to engage in a dialogue. Consider the fact that only 20 percent of what happens in class is observable. The other 80 percent is not immediately apparent and, therefore, needs to be made visible. The teacher needs to know what the learners think about the pedagogical questions concerning goals, content, methods, and media to be able to plan the next lesson at all. Teachers who rely solely on their own impression run the risk of (no longer) reaching the learners.

Successful feedback is thus a cyclic process involving two forms of feedback: feedback from the teacher to the student and feedback from the students to the teacher. Since these two forms of feedback are also structurally related and mutually dependent, it is justified to speak of an endless dialogue process that starts with correctly understood feedback.

And what about the peers? Feedback from the learners to the learners

It is without a doubt one of the most striking findings of feedback research and is also cited in Visible Learning: According to a study by Graham Nuthall (2007), most of the feedback learners give each other is incorrect. In a superficial interpretation, this finding might lead one to call into question the value of learner-to-learner feedback, and by extension also that of learner-to-teacher feedback: How are students supposed to give their teacher decent feedback if they are not even capable of giving their classmates decent feedback? But not attending to the feedback peers provide is perilous at best and can be destructive as well.

This argumentation fails to see the actual message of the study: Giving feedback is something that needs to be learned. In view of the complexity of feedback, it should be clear that it involves certain skills. For example, students need to be taught to distinguish between the levels of the task, the process, and self-regulation, and they need to develop corresponding speaking and listening skills. It helps when the students have a rubric of what the learning is meant to be for various parts of the lesson so they can optimally provide the next feedback – but this is a tall ask for teachers. And because we humans learn a lot from role models, the teacher should again play a central part in this connection.

Also important is the question of whether the person giving the feedback has the right mindframe, because this is often the reason for incorrect feedback: I refrain from telling my friend what he is doing wrong out of consideration for his feelings. I am afraid to point out where problems lie because of peer pressure. Working on improving this is a big challenge. Consequently, competence and mindframes are particularly important for successful feedback. Once the learners have acquired the necessary competence and mindframe, their teachers can successfully integrate learner-to-learner feedback into their lessons, and in a democratic school this is necessary regardless of what effects it might have.

Incidentally, all of this also goes for the teachers: We often think that fully trained teachers can do everything, but that is not the case. They are themselves still on the path to professionalization, on the path to developing the competence and the mindframe to give and demand feedback. The latter becomes an important argument particularly about the question of whether students are capable in the first place of giving their teachers feedback on their instruction. This will obviously not always be possible, but it is also a sign of expertise when teachers can use feedback at the task level to draw conclusions on the instructional process and on their own self-regulation.

An essential condition for successful feedback: a culture of mistakes

The argumentation up to this point should make it clear that a culture of mistakes is an essential condition for successful feedback: Should I see mistakes as something to avoid, or should I see them as something that is important in the learning process? Learning means making mistakes – and so does teaching.

The decision will be easy to make for teachers who take the view that focusing on shortcomings is a bad idea: They will not talk about mistakes in class, and indeed, most prefer to correct mistakes quickly and move on. Yet this also means giving up on a wide variety of learning opportunities. The mistake itself is never the problem. What can become problematic is rather the communication about the mistake: It is just as problematic to limit oneself to naming the problem – and arguing only at the task level – as it is to not name it at all. Learners often already know where they make mistakes but often are afraid to talk about them. If teachers do not allow mistakes to enter as a topic of discussion either, the result will be a culture in which mistakes are not talked about or are even glossed over. This provides a wrong message, as most of what we learn we did not know, or we may have had misconceptions or misunderstandings. Errors are opportunities for learning. The task thus must be to find a way of communicating mistakes that is on the one hand respectful toward the learners and on the other hand conducive to their learning.

Quality feedback also feeds off mistakes and misconceptions. Here again, the levels of feedback are a good place to start: It is not a good idea to provide feedback at the level of the self in response to factual mistakes. This is particularly true in the case of younger learners, because it can give them the impression that they are a failure, that they are not being capable of learning. This effect can already be observed in learners who stop receiving feedback they previously received repeatedly. For example, when learners who are used to hearing things like "Great" and "Bravo" all the time – a form of praise they perceive as being directed to the self – no longer receive such feedback, it will have a negative influence on their self-concept. In extreme cases, this can even lead to anxiety. It is, therefore, important to always make it clear to the learner what level your feedback is directed to, and once again separate out feedback about the person from feedback about the task.

Where can I start?

One of the most important steps in cultivating the mindframe "I give and help students understand feedback and I interpret and act on feedback given to me" is to take a critical look at your own feedback behavior: Am I a teacher who prefers to give feedback, or am I a teacher who prefers to demand feedback? Am I a teacher who shows students that I, too, can receive, interpret, and act on student feedback to me? Have someone listen to the levels of feedback you provide and whether there is any "where to next?" feedback in your lessons. Then it is a good idea to reflect on the levels and perspectives you prefer in giving and demanding feedback.

Use the feedback matrix below for this reflection and complete the fields in different colors – for instance red for your behavior in giving feedback and blue for your behavior in demanding feedback. Try to rate how pronounced the feedback is on a scale, for example as follows: 1 = very pronounced, 2 = moderately pronounced, and 3 = not pronounced.

You can also use this feedback matrix as an aid in planning and analyzing your lessons, for example, by integrating deliberate feedback loops into your lesson and attempting to cover all the fields on the feedback matrix. You can also use this with students when they give each other feedback. The questions listed earlier can serve as initial orientation. The goal is then to provide the optimal feedback depending where the student is in his or her learning cycle. So try to complete all the fields on the feedback matrix for a concrete case, discuss them with a colleague (or with students), implement them in your lesson, and then meet again with your colleague to discuss the results. In the same way, this method can also be used to reflect on and evaluate the feedback you gave and received in an entire lesson.

		LEVELS OF FEEDBACK		
		TASK	PROCESS	SELF-REGULATION
Perspectives of feedback	Past ("feed back")			
	Present ("feed up")			
	Future ("feed forward")			

	Task	Process	Self-regulation
Past			
Present			
Future			

If you find the feedback matrix too complex, start by focusing on just three fields – preferably those we named in the earlier example: What did the learners do right on the test, and what did they do wrong (feedback on the present at the task level)? What was the learners' learning process they were using to complete the tasks? How often did students believe that they used the right strategies to complete the task (feedback on the past at the process level)? What do the learners claim that they need to do to get a better grade on the next task? What methods should they apply to regulate their own learning process (feedback on the future at the self-regulation level)? These three questions reduce the complexity of the feedback matrix shown above.

You can also use the following questions to help in your reflection:

Task

- Does the student's answer meet the criteria for success?
- Is the answer right or wrong?
- How could the answer be expressed in greater detail?
- What is right and what is wrong about the answer?
- What does the answer lack to make it more complete?

Process

- What strategies did the student apply in the learning process?
- What was good about the learning process, and what can be improved?
- What were the student's strengths and weaknesses in the learning process?
- What further information does the way the student completed the task reveal about the learning process?
- Can the student detect the errors in his or her work?

Self-regulation

- What goals can the student regard as having reached?
- What reasons does the student give for having completed a task correctly or incorrectly?
- How does the student explain his or her success?
- What does he or she think are the next goals and the next tasks?
- How can the student self-regulate and monitor his or her learning process?
- Can they detect the errors and independently make amends to these errors?

If you discover in reflecting on your feedback practices that you tend to give more feedback than you receive, then it is high time to start focusing on the other side of the coin and trying out different methods for giving the learners opportunities to give feedback. If you are writing more than the student is writing, time to reconsider. After all, receiving feedback is ultimately even more important than giving it.

A simple example of student-to-teacher feedback is the feedback coordinate system. It maps two important aspects of instruction and can be completed by the learners (see Figure 6.8).

There are many ways you can hear your student's feedback. For example, learners who think the group work was productive and the

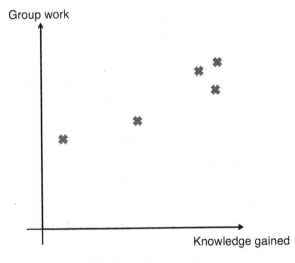

FIGURE 6.8 Feedback coordinate system

Source: Hattie and Zierer (2017).

knowledge gained was high can mark a point in the upper right-hand corner of the quadrant, while learners who think the group work was not productive and the knowledge gain was low can mark a point in the lower left-hand corner of the quadrant. This feedback is easy to collect: All you need to do is hang up the coordinate system next to the door to your classroom and ask your students to mark it when they leave. It takes only a couple of minutes, but it provides valuable information on your lesson.

This method can be adapted for use with learners who are already capable of giving more nuanced feedback, and there is also a wealth of other ideas to be discovered in the literature (see Brookhart, 2017; Wiliam & Leahy, 2015). One example is the feedback target (see Figure 6.9 for a template) (cf. Zierer, 2016b).

The feedback target might seem to paint a complete picture of feedback at first glance, but this is unfortunately not the case. For one thing, it covers only a few selected aspects of feedback and thus

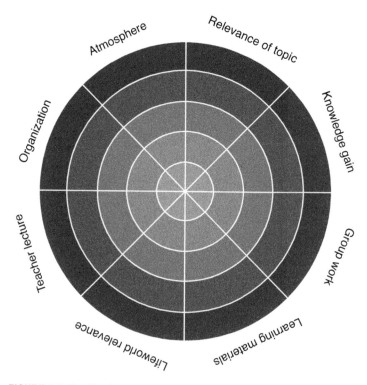

FIGURE 6.9 Feedback target

suggests a degree of completeness that is not present. As well, the individual aspects are illustrated in the shape of pie slices that make distortions inevitable: The closer the marks are to the bullseye, the less room there is for them and the closer they are to each other, and the farther the marks are from the bullseye, the more room there is for them and the farther they are from each other. It is thus necessary to discuss these issues with the learners in using the feedback target and take them into account in interpreting the results.

A less complicated way of illustrating the same feedback is with a bar chart (see Figure 6.10 for an unpopulated example).

Also worth mentioning here are methods involving new media like computers and tablets. If applied in the right way, they can bring to light information on your teaching that would otherwise be difficult or impossible to make visible – thus proving once again that new media are not effective on their own but need people to achieve the desired effect. We are having a lot of success using social media ideas to elicit student questions and feedback and to help create peer-to-peer feedback. The main advantage of new media in this context is that they are a quick and easy means of obtaining complex feedback with only little effort. For example, there are

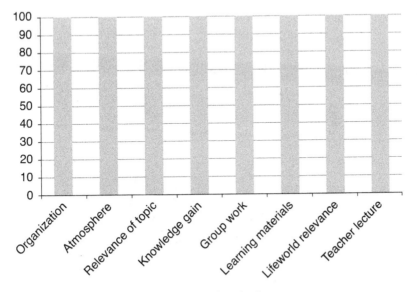

FIGURE 6.10 Feedback illustration with a bar chart

Source: Hattie and Zierer (2017).

apps available (e.g., versoapp.com, feedbackschule.de) that allow teachers to give their students detailed questionnaires and analyze the results at the click of a button, and to allow students to ask questions of each other and of the teacher. The possibilities are practically endless. However, the quality of the questions is crucial. Choose questions located at the task, process, or self-regulation levels to obtain optimal feedback on the key teaching domains of goals, content, methods, and media, as well as space and time.

It is hard to overestimate the significance of testing for achievement at the end of a lesson in this context: This is a quick way to check whether the students reached the most important goals, whether they understood the main content, whether the methods were practicable, and whether the media were useful. The test may consist of a simple crossword puzzle, but it may also be an entry in a learning journal or the homework assignment for the next class meeting, or it may involve exit tickets – this can be powerful formative information about who you have an impact on, about what, and to what extent. Chapter 2, "I see assessment as informing my impact and next steps," provides even more ideas.

CHECKLIST

Reflect on the following points next time you plan a lesson:

- Give deliberate feedback at different levels: task, process, and self-regulation depending where the student is in the learning cycle.
- Do not be stingy with feedback at the self-regulation level.
- Avoid feedback consisting of empty phrases.
- Do not mix feedback about the self with other forms of feedback.
- Give well-considered and purposeful feedback. Material rewards like candy have no place at school.
- Give feedback from various perspectives and try to link feedback on the past, present, and future.
- Harness the power of peers: Include learner-to-learner feedback in your lesson.
- Review your lesson by inviting feedback from the learners.

- Integrate phases into your lesson in which you discuss with your students whether the goals are clear, the criteria of what it means to be successful is understood, the content understandable, the methods appropriate, and the media useful.

- Determine the learning level of your students at the end of the lesson, for example by giving them a task or test. This is where you start next lesson.

- Make learning visible.

EXERCISES

- Go back to the questionnaire for self-reflection at the start of the chapter and complete it again in a different color. Where and, more important, why has your perspective on the statements changed? Discuss your self-assessment with a colleague.

- Plan your next lesson and include at least one phase each of teacher-to-learner feedback, learner-to-learner feedback, and learner-to-teacher feedback. Consult the checklist in planning this phase. Discuss your plan and the lesson with a colleague.

- Use the feedback matrix or some of the fields from it when you plan your next lesson to ensure the feedback you give is as comprehensive as possible. Discuss your plan and the lesson with a colleague.

I engage as much in dialogue as monologue

QUESTIONNAIRE FOR SELF-REFLECTION

Assess yourself by rating your agreement with the following statements: 1 = strongly disagree, 5 = strongly agree

I am very good at . . .

encouraging students to talk about content.

leading students to learning success through cooperating with others.

I know perfectly well . . .

that instructions need to be clearly formulated.

the benefits of cooperative learning methods, such as the think-pair-share principle.

My goal is always to . . .

encourage students to communicate more with each other.

encourage students to present their thinking and solution processes more often.

I'm thoroughly convinced . . .

that students should communicate with each other.

that it is important to get students to participate more often.

VIGNETTE

One of the crowning moments of teaching is to observe learners engage in a discussion about the learning material, to see them use meaningful arguments and give each other constructive criticism. At these moments, when learners become teachers, one would love nothing better than to simply lean back and listen. The power of peers comes into play and individuals experience the benefit of dialogue.

What is this chapter about?

This vignette illustrates this chapter's main message: I engage in Dialogue. This mindframe is based on exchanges with another person – whether this be other learners, the teacher, or parents.

When you finish reading this chapter, you should be able to take this message as a basis for explaining:

■ how significant the factors "classroom discussion," "peer tutoring," and "small-group learning" are.

■ what role cooperative learning can play.

■ why direct instruction is important – and different from didactic instruction.

■ why the factor "class size" is a myth within the context of the mindframe "I engage as much in dialogue as monologue."

Which factors from Visible Learning support this mindframe?

Both *Visible Learning* and *Visible Learning for Teachers* stress more than once that although teachers matter, it is how they think, how they foster students becoming their own teachers, and how they can see the impact of their efforts through the eyes of the students that matter more. The mindframe of this chapter involves teachers getting the balance right between their talking and explaining and listening and privileging student discussion. The focus is teachers listening for their impact in terms of the learning that has happened in class for their students. To listen, however, they need to not talk too much.

What percentage of the time do teachers talk in a typical class lesson? Ned Flanders (1970) spent many years studying the interaction in classrooms and developed the rule of "two-thirds." Two-thirds of classroom time someone is talking, there is a 2 out of 3 chance that this person talking is the teacher, and two-thirds of this time the teacher will be expressing his or her own opinions, lecturing, giving directions, and criticizing students. Teacher talk still dominates classrooms, with Karen Littleton et al. (2005) claiming teachers spend 70–90 percent of their teaching time "talking" and not engaging students in any discussion. Janet Clinton et al. (2014) used professional captioners to record classroom discussion across 1,500 hours in 100 classes in England, and the median was 89 percent of the talk time was by teachers.

Nystrand (1997) investigated the classroom discourse in 400 English lessons in 25 US high schools. Recitational patterns of talk were found to be overwhelmingly prevalent, and about 85 percent of the instruction observed was some combination of lecture, recitation, and seatwork. Such monological methods have a negative effect on learning. Instead, dialogically organized instruction was superior to monologically organized instruction in promoting student learning. This dialogical dialogue involved the teacher's use of authentic questions (where what counts as an acceptable answer is not prespecified), uptake conversation (where the teacher incorporates students' responses into subsequent questions), and the extent to which the teacher allows a student response to modify the topic of discourse. These three strategies form the basis of dialogic teaching.

Dialogic teaching aims to stimulate and extend student thinking, allowing the student and teacher to more precisely diagnose what they know and misunderstand, such that the next learning task can be most appropriately framed. It privileges students thinking aloud. It is not the usual question-answer, tell-practice, and listen-tell routines. It highlights, however, that it is not so much the amount of talk that matters, but the nature of the dialogue. It involves not merely listening to what they say, but demonstrating that you have listened and understood what they are saying. It is a way of thinking about how to teach via listening, prompting, and reacting to how students are thinking. Robin Alexander and Michael Armstrong (2010) term this "scaffolded dialogue," which involves:

- *interactions*, which encourage children to think, and to think in different ways.

- *questions*, which require much more than simple recall.
- *answers*, which are followed up and built on rather than merely received.
- *feedback*, which informs and leads thinking forward as well as encourages.
- *contributions*, which are extended rather than fragmented.
- *exchanges*, which chain together into coherent and deepening lines of enquiry.
- *classroom organization, climate, and relationships*, which make all this possible.
- *uptake*, (one person responding to and taking forward the ideas of another).
- *scaffolding*, (providing the child with an appropriate linguistic and/ or conceptual tool to bridge the gap between present and intended understanding).
- *handover*, (successful transfer of what is to be learned and assimilation of new learning to existing knowledge and understanding).

This is what we mean by "I engage in as much dialogue as monologue," and it is a dialogue not only between teachers and students, but also between students, and between students and their parents.

In the following, we present major factors that relate to engaging dialogue: "classroom discussions," "peer tutoring," and "small-group learning."

Classroom discussion

"Classroom discussion" is one of the factors that was added with the expansion of the database between the publication of *Visible Learning* and *Visible Learning for Teachers*. It achieves an effect size of 0.82, thus breaking right into the top-ranked factors at seventh place (see Figure 7.1). What does this method involve, and why is it so successful? Classroom discussions are characterized by the fact that (a) they involve a high degree of student activity, (b) the questions and problems of learners become visible through spoken dialogue in the learning process, (c) learners receive feedback from teachers, and (d) teachers receive many kinds of feedback on their instruction from students. In this way, classroom discussions combine several factors that lead to large effects. Their key feature is thus dialogue,

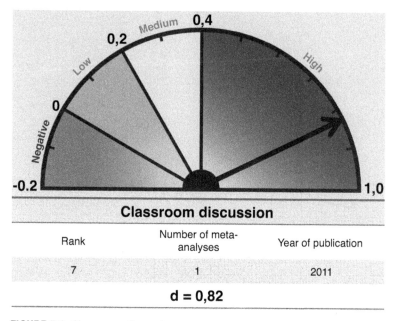

Classroom discussion

Rank	Number of meta-analyses	Year of publication
7	1	2011

d = 0,82

FIGURE 7.1 Classroom discussion

Source: Hattie and Zierer (2017).

exploration of the learning material in oral form, and thinking aloud. In more recent studies, Hattie and Donoghue (2016) showed that the optimal time for classroom discussion is after students have sufficient surface level content knowledge such that are ready to make connections between ideas, explore what they do and do not know, and try to transfer their knowledge to various contexts. Thus, classroom discussion is not a method that can be applied in every situation, and it depends on the learners and their current learning level, particularly their skills concerning the material to be learned and their powers of articulation. It is, nevertheless, clearly one of the most influential methods in regard to fostering self-regulation and deep understanding.

Peer tutoring

Programs in which learners assume the role of teachers and thus become tutors have been shown consistently to have a major impact on the learning performance of all involved – that is, both the students being taught and the students doing the teaching. We are sure most teachers know how they learn so much more preparing to

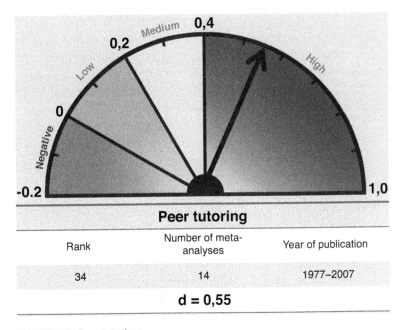

Peer tutoring

Rank	Number of meta-analyses	Year of publication
34	14	1977–2007

d = 0,55

FIGURE 7.2 Peer tutoring

Source: Hattie and Zierer (2017).

teach than sitting in a room listening to others talk to them. But, too often, they forget this when, after preparation, they walk into a class and talk and talk and talk. In Visible Learning, peer tutoring has an effect size of 0.55 (see Figure 7.2). The most important qualification to this finding is that peer tutoring should not serve as a replacement for the teacher, because then the influence rapidly wanes and can even turn negative – particularly if the level of challenge has been set too high. Accordingly, such programs should be a complement to the activities of the teacher, who has the oversight of seeing that the goals are clear, the processes for the teaching by the students are transparent, peer tutors know how to evaluate their impact, and there are reasonable directions for the peers to work within. Hence, in peer tutoring too, learning turns out to be a dialogic process in which learners are not just passive consumers of instruction but always also producers of learning.

Small-group learning

The challenging task faced by the teacher of first initiating dialogic processes in school and instruction and then making them successful may be illustrated by the factor "small-group learning." It has an effect size of 0.49 – in apparent contradiction to similar factors that concern the size of the learning group (see Figure 7.3): Reducing "class size" achieves an effect size of only 0.21, and "within-class grouping," which involves splitting a class up into groups for an extended period without reference to a learning task, makes it only to 0.18. How can these differences be explained, and what is the reason for them? A look at what these latter two factors lack demonstrates why the former is so much more influential: The latter are more structural changes and, too often, the structure (reducing class size, membership of groups) become all important and the nature of the teaching is not altered as a consequence of the different structure. For example, if you reduce the class size from 30 to 15 and still teach the same way, it should be no surprise that the effects are small; indeed, given that "tell and practice" is a dominant teaching method in classes of 25–30, it should be less of a surprise that teachers use "tell and practice" more in smaller classes: where they talk more in smaller classes, there

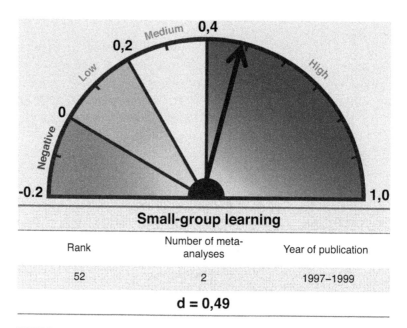

Small-group learning

Rank	Number of meta-analyses	Year of publication
52	2	1997–1999

d = 0,49

FIGURE 7.3 Small-group learning

Source: Hattie and Zierer (2017).

is less group work, there is less feedback (Hattie, 2009). The success of within-class group learning (rather than reducing classes or tracking or streaming classes) is that teaching has particular aims, which are temporary and can be rebuilt with different students depending on the aim, and require teachers to build structure for any small-group task. Within-class group learning can optimize the opportunities for enhanced dialogue. The success of within-class groups formed within a school or a class depend crucially on whether teachers have the mindframe to move from monologue to privileging dialogue and to design their lessons accordingly.

Cooperative learning: harnessing the power of peers

The factor "cooperative learning" merits special consideration, because learning together might be expected to foster the mindframe "I engage in as much dialogue as monologue."

To begin, it should be noted that there are several Visible Learning factors involving cooperative learning. One of them compares cooperative vs. individualistic learning (d = 0.59), a second compares cooperative vs. competitive learning (d = 0.54), and a third compares competitive vs. individualistic learning (d = 0.24). Hence, the results are clear: Cooperative learning is superior to both competitive learning and individualized learning, and competitive learning achieves larger effects than individualized learning. There are some important findings on cooperative learning that are worth noting.

First, studies have demonstrated that the effect size of cooperative learning increases as learners get older. This suggests that cooperative learning is something that must be learned. Too often, students are placed in groups as if they then know what to do to maximize the benefits for themselves and the whole group. So often students are placed in cooperative groups but spend most of the time then working on individual activities. Everyone who has taught at an elementary school knows how difficult it is to get elementary school students to concentrate, raise their hands to answer questions, and sit still, let alone work together. This is not to say that the idea of cooperative learning in elementary school is not appropriate. On the contrary, the foundation for successful cooperative learning in later years can be laid in elementary school. Incidentally, this is true of every method: The more experience learners have with a method, the more effective it can be.

Second, studies also indicate that cooperative learning is hardly any more effective than other methods for certain tasks, such as memorization and the completion of homework assignments. Thus, the influence of cooperative learning decreases for tasks that can be completed without a dialogic structure. In our recent synthesis of factors that relate to "how we learn," we argued that successful cooperative learning is more likely after students have acquired the surface or content information. When they know much, when the student is ready to make links in their ideas, when they are in a state of cognitive conflict, when they have two or more ideas that make sense to them but when compared side by side appear to conflict with each other, when they need to identify contradictions, when they are in a state of disequilibrium, when they want to test hypotheses, or when they are ready to falsify some of their older thinking – this is all dependent on knowing much.

Third, there are skills that can be developed to maximize the working among colleagues (and this applies to students as well as teachers). There is the claim that there is wisdom in the crowd, but the research suggests some key attributes are needed for the group to produce outcomes greater than the mere sum of contributions made by each individual. For example, when the tasks are made up of discrete, factual items (e.g., a pub quiz or game show) they tend to lend themselves more readily to a "truth wins" scenario where the group's brightest members will often prove more dominant than others in providing answers to closed questions. However, when group tasks require considered negotiation and judgment (e.g., Is the plaintiff guilty or innocent?), mere factual exchanges are insufficient and the importance of the "brightest" member is superseded by those who contribute more to the harmonious function of the group. Such members are more "group-minded" than "truth-minded" and tend to be high on personality traits such as "conscientiousness" and cognitive abilities that go beyond IQ, such as "social sensitivity" – the ability to read and rapidly adjust to emotional cues, listen to others, and steer viewpoints away from circular conflict and toward productive cohesion.

These findings to increase the value of collaborative grouping point to the importance of creating dialogue among students, teaching them how to work in groups, and reducing the amount of teacher talk to allow peers to articulate their thoughts and understanding so that the teacher can hear his or her impact and for students to listen, interpret, and test their ideas.

Direct instruction: the complement to cooperative learning

Direct instruction is near the top of the ranking, with an effect size of 0.59, but it is very misunderstood. Because there are as many myths circulating around about the factor "direct instruction" as there are about the factor "cooperative learning," it is important to take a closer look. This is particularly important given so often direct instruction is misinterpreted as teachers talking, following scripts built by others, and mechanically following a set of recipes. Indeed, this is not direct instruction. The distinguishing features of direct instruction include the following:

1. There is a clear idea of what the *learning intentions* of the lesson are.

2. The teacher needs to know, and the students informed, what *success criteria* of performance are to be expected and when and what students will be held accountable for from the lesson/activity.

3. There is a need to *build commitment and engagement* in the learning task.

4. The teacher should present the lesson using modeling, checking for understanding, and providing worked examples.

5. There is much *guided practice*; the opportunity for each student to demonstrate his or her grasp of new learning by working through an activity or exercise while the teacher provides feedback and individual remediation as needed.

6. There is the *closure* to the lesson, whereby students are helped to bring things together in their own minds, to make sense out of what has just been taught.

7. There is *independent practice* – probably the most critical part often omitted when implementing direct instruction.

The list reveals the differences between direct instruction and didactic instruction and highlights the significance of dialogue for the former: Achieving clarity about the goals and content of the lesson as well as the use of methods and media involves not just clear ideas on the part of the teacher, but also and especially, intensive phases of exchange, cooperation, and confrontation between the teacher and the learners. And it is precisely this effort that leads in cases of success to corresponding clarity in the latter. It does seem ironic that many educators despise direct instruction (again, often mistaking it for didactic teaching), preferring their own monological methods of "tell and practice"; they prefer their own voice to a method that is among the most powerful on student learning. Maybe direct instruction needs a name change, as it has accrued so much negative press. Some are calling it explicit instruction, systematic direct instruction, and others differentiate between capital DI and lowercase di. Our claim is that the previous seven attributes conjointly are powerful, and therefore we call this combination the more neutral "deliberate teaching and learning" (DTL).

DTL is, therefore, a type of instruction in which both the teacher and the learners know precisely who is supposed to do what, when, why, how, and where and with whom they are supposed to do it. In the manner of a stage director or conductor, the teacher guides the learners through the lesson with a skillful use of methodology yet, at the same time, gives the students a chance to become active themselves in their learning. To implement DTL, dialogue is privileged, and teachers must become excellent listeners and, as important, show the students that they are excellent listeners. The success of DTL lies in achieving an understanding between the teacher and the learners about the goals, the content, the methods, and their progress (i.e., progress of both the students and teacher). In other words, the clarity of the teacher comes into contact with the clarity of the learners and the interaction between the two leads to instruction that is also marked by clarity.

Class size: important but not necessary for dialogue

To be clear right from the outset, we are for smaller classes because they can make many things possible that are particularly effective. The summary of research in Visible Learning shows the overall effect from reducing class size is positive (about .20). This means that reducing class size enhances achievement; that is what a positive effect size means. The questions are threefold: Why is this effect so small relative to the many other effects? Should we spend the millions to further reduce class size instead of spending these millions on enhancing teacher expertise? How can we enhance the size of this effect?

A major reason why the effect is so small is to study what happens when teachers are placed in larger classes (typically 25–30 students) compared with these same teachers placed in smaller classes (15–20 students). As we noted earlier, in larger classes there is a dominance of "tell and practice" (which, as noted in Visible Learning, has worked overall), and when these teachers are placed in smaller classes they enact even more tell and practice. They do not change their methods to optimize the opportunities in smaller classes. A major reason why the overall effect is about .20 is that students can no longer hide and escape the effects of instruction in smaller classes – so it seems ironic that the positive effect is more a function of students than teachers changing what they do.

A summary of the research considering classrooms of differing sizes shows that there are no differences in the percentage of student-initiated questions, the percentage of student-initiated comments, the percentage of students off task, in time waiting for help in reading or mathematics, classroom climate, text coverage, time working with individual students, or on administrative tasks. There were very small effects for reducing disruptive behaviors. There was more whole-class teaching and more time on lesson review and less individualization in smaller classes, fewer teacher-student interactions, and fewer student questions. There were no differences in students' attitudes toward school, for their self-concepts, or for their participation in classroom tasks (cf. Hattie, 2009).

We could retrain teachers to optimize the opportunities in smaller classes. For example, if we used the fewer number of students to maximize dialogue, then it is likely we could see more positive effects, but that would entail a radical change in how we teach for many educators. And, not surprisingly, if there is less monologue and more dialogue, this can occur regardless of the number of students in the class. It is the dialogue that matters.

We are by no means suggesting here that a reduction in class size is pointless or that class sizes can be increased at will – that would be another example of a misinterpretation of the evidence as the effect size for class size reduction is positive, indicating that reducing class sizes does enhance outcomes (just not by much). What we are suggesting is rather if teachers do not take advantage of structural changes to do things differently, reducing class size will have (and has not had) little impact. However, if teachers succeed in using these structural changes for more intensive dialogue, then the outcomes may be more enhanced.

Where can I start?

There is hardly a field as diverse as that of finding ways to enhance the levels of dialogue in classrooms. The possibilities are practically endless, including everything from group puzzles, jigsaw methods, fishbowl to placemat activities – and new ideas are being introduced all the time. Spicing up your lessons with cooperative learning elements is, therefore, a good place to start – with the aim of maximizing student dialogue in a structured and considered manner: to involve all in the group as part of this dialogue and to evaluate the impact of dialogue on student learning and understanding. The important thing to remember here, too, however, is that it is not just a matter of choosing a method. What is even more important is to verify that the method you chose was indeed successful. In other words, your keyword should be evidence of learning and your guiding principle "Know thy impact."

A common form of cooperative learning in the English-speaking world is the think-pair-share strategy. It involves three phases: In the first phase (think), the learners come up with individual ideas about a topic on their own. In the second phase (pair), they get together in small groups to discuss and compare their ideas. Finally, in the third phase (share), they present the results from the second phase to the entire class.

Consider also the following methods of collaborative grouping to maximize the power to enhance learning dialogue.

Jigsaw activity (d = 1.09)

Just as in a jigsaw puzzle, each piece – each student's part – is essential for the completion and full understanding of the final product. If each student's part is essential, then each student is essential, and that is precisely what makes this strategy so effective (www.jigsaw. org/#overview). To illustrate one way that jigsaw can be used, imagine a task where we have five readings based on five influences from the *Visible Learning* book (a task we often use in our own workshops).

1. Sit at tables of five. Agree who is A, B, C, D, and E.

2. Person A reads and makes notes on one of the influences (e.g., classroom discussion), B on teacher clarity, C on collaborative grouping, D on direct instruction, and E on class size (about 12 minutes).

3. All the As then meet (and the Bs meet, etc.) to talk about the underlying story, what are the main messages, and so forth (about 15–20 minutes). The value is that all students, regardless of ability, can teach and learn from each other about the content and ideas for each influence.

4. The students then return to original group and report back the major findings and understandings to the others. So, now, there are five sets of ideas and understandings for each group. The major

purpose of this step is to see connections between the major ideas across the five influences.

5. Each group then shares their major ideas, and a whole-group discussion is held to ensure all understand the major themes underlying these five successful practices.

6. Each group then considers one or two (only) of some lesson plans provided. The task is to consider the content and delivery of the lesson plans in relation to what you have learned from these influences. What are the strengths, and what might you change based on the findings related to these influences?

Group puzzle

Group puzzle involves first dividing the class up into expert groups, each of which is responsible for preparing a different aspect of the topic treated in the lesson. Then the groups are rearranged, with at least one member representing each expert group. In the new groups, the learners report on and discuss the results from the expert groups (see Figure 7.4).

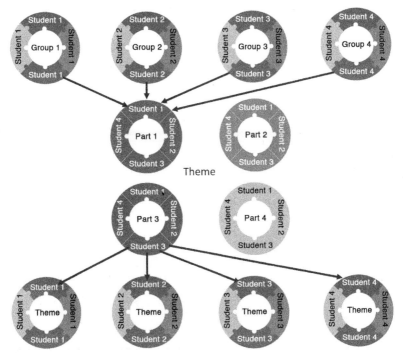

FIGURE 7.4 Group puzzle

Source: Hattie and Zierer (2017).

Fishbowl

The class is divided up into an inner and an outer circle. The students in the inner circle have the task of discussing a topic assigned by the teacher, while those in the outer circle function as observers. Members of the inner circle may decide to switch to the outer circle and vice versa (see Figure 7.5).

Placemat activity

After dividing the class up into groups of four, the teacher asks the learners to first work on a problem alone and write down their solution on one of the edges of a placemat. Then each member of the group reads the solutions suggested by the other members and engages in a discussion about them. The group agrees on a common solution and writes it down in the middle of the placemat (see Figure 7.6).

Harness this great spectrum of possibilities to integrate cooperative learning into your lessons and use dialogue. Always keep in mind that these methods are no surefire recipe for success but only have been shown in the past to produce positive effects on student learning with a certain likelihood. By no means does this relieve you of

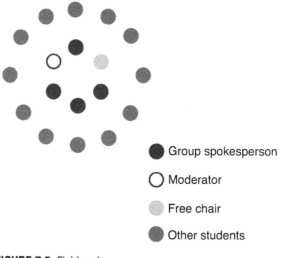

● Group spokesperson

○ Moderator

● Free chair

● Other students

FIGURE 7.5 Fishbowl

Source: Hattie and Zierer (2017).

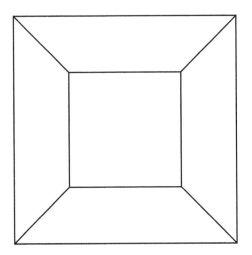

FIGURE 7.6 Placemat activity

Source: Hattie and Zierer (2017).

the responsibility of looking for evidence that the method you chose was also successful in your own lesson. We provided tips on doing so in Chapter 6, "I give and help students understand feedback and I interpret and act on feedback given to me."

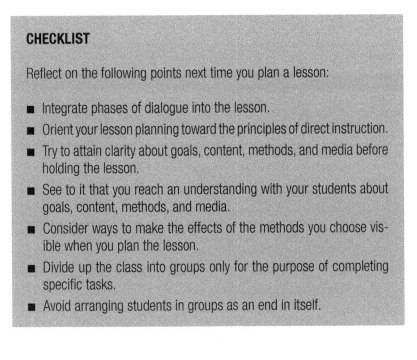

CHECKLIST

Reflect on the following points next time you plan a lesson:

- Integrate phases of dialogue into the lesson.
- Orient your lesson planning toward the principles of direct instruction.
- Try to attain clarity about goals, content, methods, and media before holding the lesson.
- See to it that you reach an understanding with your students about goals, content, methods, and media.
- Consider ways to make the effects of the methods you choose visible when you plan the lesson.
- Divide up the class into groups only for the purpose of completing specific tasks.
- Avoid arranging students in groups as an end in itself.

- Harness the power of peers through cooperative learning forms.
- Make sure to integrate targeted input phases. They are important for preparing, introducing, commenting on, reinforcing, and following up on phases of dialogue.

EXERCISES

- Go back to the questionnaire for self-reflection at the start of the chapter and complete it again in another color. Where and, more important, why has your perspective on the statements changed? Discuss your self-assessment with a colleague.
- Plan your next lesson and include a phase of cooperative learning. Obtain feedback on it from your learners. Discuss your plan, the lesson, and the feedback with a colleague.
- Compare your lesson plan with the features of direct instruction presented in this chapter and modify points you find lacking in clarity. Discuss these modifications with a colleague.

I explicitly inform students what successful impact looks like from the outset

---

QUESTIONNAIRE FOR SELF-REFLECTION

Assess yourself by rating your agreement with the following statements: 1 = strongly disagree, 5 = strongly agree

I am very good at . . .

showing the learner what the goal of the lesson is.

showing the learner what the success criteria of learning are.

I know perfectly well . . .

that learning needs clear, challenging, and transparent goals.

that the visibility of the success criteria is an essential aid for learners.

My goal is always to . . .

make the objectives of teaching clear, challenging, and transparent.

show learners the success criteria.

I am thoroughly convinced . . .

that it is my job to ensure clear, challenging, and transparent goals.

that the visibility of success criteria is important for learners.

VIGNETTE

Who does not know the following situation: The teacher quickly and vaguely explains the group work and disappears from the classroom while the learners are left alone and the task is to be solved. They try to figure out what the actual goal of the group work is and what will constitute success of their efforts. At last, after a long search, they agree, and the teacher comes back and asks for the learning result. The students do not have any answers because they did not have time to work on the goals. How differently would the described lesson have run if the teacher had taken time at the beginning and made clear to the learners what they should learn and why and what for, and what the goal of the next steps is. The conversation about it would not lead to silence but would make learning visible.

This vignette is intended to illustrate the core message of this chapter: Successful learning requires clarity – not only in the learning process but also in view of the learning outcome. The better teachers in the classroom are able to demonstrate the success criteria to the learners, the more effective and lasting the efforts on the part of the learners will be.

After reading this chapter, you should be able to explain, in light of this core message:

■ the extent to which the factors "worked examples" and "mastery learning" are significant.

■ the importance of learning objectives and success criteria for visible learning and successful teaching.

■ what is meant by the Visible Learning Wheel and what possibilities exist for implementing it.

Which factors from Visible Learning support this mindframe?

It is an ongoing discussion: When in the learning process is it necessary to inform learners about the success criteria of the lessons? The positions are far apart: On the one hand, there are arguments that learning requires a stress curve in order to motivate and have a sustained effect, so it is better to let learners grope in the dark for as long as possible. On the other hand, some advocate showing learners as early as possible during the learning process what the goal is and what constitutes learning success.

In the following, we defend neither position, because the timing depends on the goal of the lesson: If, for example, problem solving itself is the focus, goal fulfillment may become explicit later, while it is evident much earlier in the process of teaching simple facts. However, the results of empirical research indicate that it is necessary at a certain time in the classroom to make the success criteria visible to the learner and make them the explicit object of the discussion. For learners, it is doubtlessly helpful to know when they have reached the learning goal and the success criteria. Teaching in which the success criteria of learning are not brought up is a lost opportunity.

As a result, there are certainly several ways to reach the learning goal. But the disclosure of the success criteria no later than when the goal is achieved is essential for successful and sustainable learning. Against this background, the attitude "I explicitly inform students what successful impact looks like from the outset" seems to be essential for successful teaching. In Visible Learning, there are a number of factors that underpin what has been said.

Worked examples

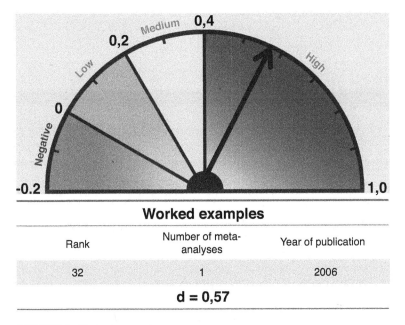

Worked examples

Rank	Number of meta-analyses	Year of publication
32	1	2006

d = 0,57

FIGURE 8.1 Worked examples

Source: Hattie and Zierer (2017).

Showing learners worked examples is an effective method for learning goal and success demonstration. In general, worked examples contain the problem description and the appropriate solution steps and are presented in three parts: (1) an introduction phase (presentation of the example), (2) an elaboration or training phase (follow-up of the solution path), and (3) a test phase (assessment of learning). Through this structured process oriented toward the learning goal, worked examples reduce cognitive stress for the learners. They can focus on the process that leads to the correct answer, as opposed to giving a simple answer that can be right or wrong. As a result, the focus is placed on the identification of learning outcomes and success criteria, which can lead to challenges.

By providing worked examples, the teacher reduces the means-end search; that is, students focus more on the problem and the steps in the process, and thus are more likely to induce generalized solutions or schemas. The attention is not whether the answers are right or wrong or whether the desired level of performance has been attained, but on the process of learning. Zhu and Simon (1987) reported across a number of long-term studies that worked examples could increase learning by 1.5 times the conventional classes where worked examples were not provided. Paas and Van Merriënboer (1994) found worked examples in teacher geometry problem solving yielded lower demands on cognitive load, better schema construction, and higher transfer performance.

Mastery learning

The basic idea of the Mastery Learning approach is that all children can learn something when they are provided with adequate explanations regarding the understanding and mastery of the subject to be learned. Mastery learning typically involves demanding that students achieve a specified level of mastery (e.g., 85 percent in a vocabulary test) before moving forward to learn new and subsequent information. It entails copious feedback and clear success criteria and can become a virtuous cycle of teaching and learning – provided the learning remains interesting and appropriately challenging. It can be powerful aiding differentiation, as what varies is less the level of mastery but the time and way students can attain this mastery. It also focuses on the teachers' skill in teaching and knowing their impact on student learning such that they can adjust their teaching to assist students attain the level of mastery. Not saying "good work, it is good

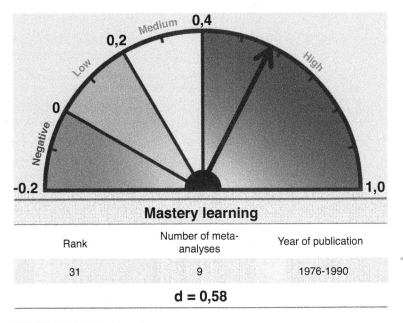

Mastery learning

Rank	Number of meta-analyses	Year of publication
31	9	1976-1990

d = 0,58

FIGURE 8.2 Mastery learning

Source: Hattie and Zierer (2017).

enough" as both the student and teacher are aware of the level of mastery, but it certainly can take much preparation to ensure the level is appropriate and the structures and time are in place to allow for learning to mastery and very personalized cycles of learning by students.

The effects of mastery testing are particularly strong on lower ability students, primarily because it increases the amount of instructional time required by, on average, 25 percent for these students. Bloom (1984) argued that although students can vary widely in their learning rates, if teachers could provide the appropriate time and the most defensible learning conditions, nearly all students can reach appropriately challenging success criteria (see Guskey, 2010).

Goals and success criteria: eyes like twins

The results so far point to an interaction that is essential for successful teaching: Learning objectives and success criteria are two sides of a coin and are mutually dependent on each other regarding their effect. The explication of the one criterion is, therefore, worthwhile especially when the other criterion is also made visible. The difference between the two is that learning objectives, at the beginning of the learning process, reveal what the goal of learning is and success criteria are made visible when this learning goal is reached and the learner can see that he has reached the learning goal.

Against this background, it is important not only for teachers to know what the goal of the lesson is and when it has been achieved but also to share this knowledge with the learner and to make it the explicit subject of the lesson.

The following overview tries to illustrate the interactions and the interrelations between learning objectives and success criteria. For this purpose, a teaching example is selected and worked through using the SOLO model, which has already been addressed in Chapter 5 (cf. Hattie, 2012).

Learning intentions success criteria

SOLO 1: RECOGNIZE THAT LIGHT AND SOUND ARE TYPES OF ENERGY THAT ARE DETECTED BY EARS AND EYES

Unistructural/ multistructural	Recognize that light/ sound are forms of energy and have properties	I can name one or more properties of light/ sound	❏
Relational	Know that sound/light can be transformed into other forms of energy	I can explain how light/sound is transformed into other types of energy	❏
Extended abstract	Understand how light/ sound allows us to communicate	I can discuss how light/sound enables us to communicate	❏

SOLO 2: BE ABLE TO DRAW A NORMAL, MEASURE ANGLES, AND DEFINE THE LAW OF REFLECTION

Unistructural/ multistructural	Be able to draw ray diagrams, including the normal, with correctly drawn angles	I can draw a ray diagram with correctly measured angles	❏

(Continued)

Relational	Be able to define the Law of Reflection, linking the terms "incidence" and "reflected ray"	I can define the Law of Reflection, linking the terms "incidence" and "reflected ray," "normal" and "smooth surface"	❏
Extended abstract	Recognize that the Law of Reflection is true for all plane surfaces and can predict what will happen if the surface is rough	I can predict what will happen if light is reflected off a rough surface and explain why it happens	❏

SOLO 3: BE ABLE TO USE RAY BOXES TO UNDERSTAND HOW CONCAVE AND CONVEX MIRRORS BEHAVE

Unistructural/ multi-structural	Know that changing the distance of an object from a concave mirror changes the appearance of the image	I can recognize that an image in a concave mirror changes as an object is moved closer or farther away from the mirror	❏
Relational	Be able to explain why concave mirrors are known as "converging mirrors" and convex mirrors as "diverging mirrors"	I can explain (using diagrams) why concave and convex mirrors are referred to as "converging" and "diverging" mirrors, respectively	❏
Extended abstract	Recognize patterns in reflected rays from concave and convex mirrors, and be able to make a generalization	I can write a generalization about the patterns of reflected rays in concave and convex mirrors	❏

This example demonstrates what has been shown in empirical studies, that l objectives and success criteria are crucial for learning success and lead to five didactic implications:

First, challenge: Visibility of learning objectives and addressing the success criteria lead to the fact that learners can better understand where they are in the learning process, where they have their strengths and weaknesses, and where the dissonance between the can-do and the cannot-yet-do lies. Improperly understood, this can lead to tension on the part of the learner – especially when personal and non-performance-related aspects are at the center of instruction. The focus on the subject and the learning object can provide a remedy and can put dealing with errors into the proper perspective.

Second, self-commitment: The visualization of learning objectives and the discussion of success criteria are important in order to make learners responsible for their learning. The better this succeeds, the greater the learning success. In addition to the challenge already mentioned, it is social contacts and peer influences that lead to high self-commitment.

Third, self-confidence: Trust in one's own ability is important for learning success. This is the result of self-efficacy beliefs on the one hand and social contact on the other. Above all, teachers have the opportunity to show learners what they are already able to do and where they have already made progress by making learning objectives visible and addressing the success criteria. On this basis, challenges can be posed, which can be mastered by the learners and do not overburden or challenge them.

Fourth, the expectations of the learner: The visualization of learning objectives and addressing the success criteria helps learners to assess themselves – in the sense that they learn to develop realistic expectations of themselves. All this is not an easy path but requires many conversations and reflections. It is nevertheless a hallmark of successful learners.

Fifth, conceptual understanding: Learning moves from a superficial understanding to a deep understanding. Neither is more important nor better than the other. Rather, the one builds on the other and thus shows their interaction. Understanding this interaction is what is called conceptual understanding. Learners who know at what level they are, why this level is important, and what their next steps are can learn more effectively and sustainably. The visibility of learning objectives and the discussion of success criteria is an important tool for teachers.

Where can I start?

In 2015, a multipart documentary showed across Australia called "Revolution School" about a school development process caused headlines: Kambrya College set out to turn from one of the worst schools in Australia to one of the best. Founded in 2002 in Berwick, just 50 kilometers from Melbourne, the school now has more than 1,000 students, of which over 25 percent have a migration background and represent more than 35 nationalities – a typical school in the 21st century, if you will. In 2008, the school was flagged as a "red school" – low achievement and low progress. So the school management team, headed by principal Michael Muscat, set out to contact, among others, the Graduate School of the University of Melbourne. During this exchange, numerous strategies were developed and procedures implemented to help the school progress. After a short time, it was possible to reform the school and bring it to success. This success was nearly all a function of the leadership team and the dedication and passion of the teachers. They used the research, they implemented and refined, and the relentlessly evaluated their impact. Of the multitude of interventions, we single out one in the context of these considerations that can clarify the core idea of the mindframe as a first step toward a corresponding professionalization:

In an intensive exchange process, the teaching staff agreed to make central factors of successful teaching in the classroom visible and to focus on them again and again. The decision was made to focus on the factors "goals" and "success criteria." Of course, one could also name other factors. What is much more important, however, is first the underlying process whereby the staff discussed learning success and teaching quality, and second, the agreement to make this understanding the principle of all instruction. Classroom quality is thus visible not only to the teachers, but also and above all to the learners. The goal that the school set for itself is not an easy one, but it is a lesson in evidence orientation: no more lessons in which the learners are not clear why they are learning something. No more lessons in which the learner is not shown what the success criteria are. And no more lessons in which learners do not know what media they are using and for what purpose.

Ultimately, this communication process and the resulting understanding of teaching provided a guarantee for the success of Kambrya College. The college went from the bottom 10 percent in the state to the top 20 percent. Collective expectations of efficiency led to profound changes. We see in this process and in the agreement on the described instrument an evidence-based path that is worth taking.

So talk to your colleagues. Define success criteria about the lessons, which then become binding for you and visible to the learners.

Place these success criteria at a central place in the classroom – not on the sidelines – and refer to them throughout the lesson. Make learning visible and create challenges, self-commitment, trust, reasonable expectations, and conceptual understanding. In this way, you are making a decisive step toward implementing the mindframe "I explicitly inform students what successful impact looks like from the outset." The following overview, which we call the Visible Learning Wheel against the background of the Kambrya College, can be helpful (see Figure 8.3).

One comment is necessary at this point to avoid misunderstandings: The Visible Learning Wheel is not to be considered a corset, but an expression of collective professionalization, and therefore a fundamental attitude of the teaching staff. For learners, it also leads to a visualization of learning and teaching, and this is the ultimate reason.

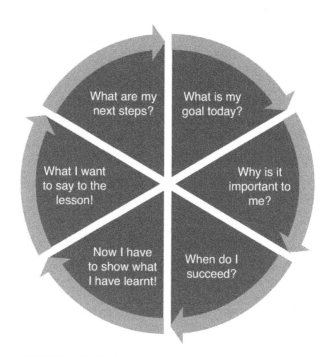

FIGURE 8.3 Visible Learning Wheel

CHECKLIST

- Always formulate appropriate success criteria for the objectives of the lesson.
- Make the success criteria visible in the learning process and name them.
- In the learning process, introduce case studies to make both the learning goal and the success criteria of learning visible.
- Complete each lesson with the goal of revising the learning objectives and addressing the success criteria.
- Make sure that the learner understands the success criteria by requesting feedback.

EXERCISES

- Return to the self-reflection questionnaire at the beginning of the chapter and fill it in with a different color. Where has your view of things changed and, above all, why? Discuss your assessments with a colleague.
- Plan your next lesson including a worked example. Discuss your planning and implementation with a colleague.
- Design a Visible Learning Wheel with your colleagues and discuss its benefit with the learner from a learning perspective. Discuss your experiences with your colleagues and develop this tool on an evidence-based basis.

I build relationships and trust so that learning can occur in a place where it is safe to make mistakes and learn from others

build trust among my students.

I'm thoroughly convinced ...

that a positive relationship with my students is important.

that it is important to establish a fair and positive climate in the class.

VIGNETTE

There are only very few children who do not have any fear when they have to make their first presentation in a class. There are not many options available to a teacher in situations like this. The student can say "I'm anxious," "What if I forgot my words?" "What if I fail?" "What if my classmates laugh at me?" or "I can't do it" – and all these comments can signal that they need help. It makes no difference how painstakingly the teacher discussed the presentation with the child beforehand – all theory goes out the window when the time comes to perform. The child needs an atmosphere of confidence and trust, an atmosphere that gives him or her a feeling of security so that the child can make the presentation.

What is this chapter about?

This vignette illustrates this chapter's main message: Learning requires positive relationships – whether between learners and teachers, or between learners and their peers. Instruction is, therefore, essentially built on a relationship building, and the more safe and trusting these relationships are, the more the child will learn. These positive relationships are the precursors to learning – they form a resource to be spent when in challenging situations – as then students need to feel much trust to ask for help, to try again, and explore openly with their peers.

When you finish reading this chapter, you should be able to take this message as a basis for explaining:

■ how significant the factors "teacher expectations," "teacher-student relationships," and "reducing anxiety" are.

■ what significance the IKEA effect has on the development of intact teacher-student relationships.

- why a "not yet" is always better than a "not" for strengthening teacher–student relationships.

- why humor and cheerfulness should have a place in school and the classroom and how they can improve teacher-student relationships.

- what the chameleon effect is and what impact rules and rituals have on establishing and maintaining intact teacher-student relationships.

- why the teacher's credibility is a key to positive teacher-student relationships.

Which factors from Visible Learning support this mindframe?

The notion that learning needs an atmosphere of security, trust, and confidence and not an atmosphere of fear and repression is by no means new. One need only think of Johann Friedrich Herbart's (1808) "pedagogical rhythm," Herman Nohl's (1970) "pedagogical reference," or even Otto Friedrich Bollnow's (2001) "pedagogical love." All these concepts stress how important the teacher-student relationship is for successful learning.

In the following, we present major factors that relate to developing positive relations: "teacher expectations," "teacher-student relationships," and "reducing anxiety."

Teacher expectations

The effect size of 0.43 for "teacher expectations" in Visible Learning should make us sit up and take notice (see Figure 9.1).

One of the more famous experiments in education was conducted by Rosenthal and Jacobsen, called the Pygmalion effect. Pygmalion was a Greek sculptor who fell in love with a statue of a beautiful women he carved. He kissed and doted on the statue, which then turned into a woman, and his expectations were realized. Similarly, Rosenthal and Jacobsen told teachers that half their students would "bloom" during the year and half would not – based on tests that they have administered (but the division into the bloomers group was random). Sure enough, at the end of the year, more bloomers outperformed non-bloomers. Given the assignment was random, the difference they claimed was a function of the higher expectations of the teachers about these bloomers.

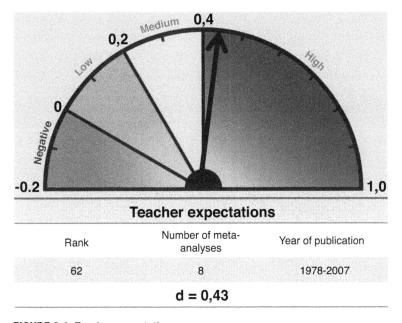

Teacher expectations

Rank	Number of meta-analyses	Year of publication
62	8	1978-2007

d = 0,43

FIGURE 9.1 Teacher expectations

Source: Hattie and Zierer (2017).

This led to much hunting for the sources of these expectations – gender, ethnicity, social class, stereotypes, diagnostic labels, physical attractiveness, language style, the age of the student, personality and social skills, the relationship between teacher and student background, names, other siblings, and one-parent background. None of these really succeeded in explaining the source of teacher expectations. Christine Rubie-Davies (2016) argued that this hunt was based on a misunderstanding; as the most important implication was that teachers who had high expectations tended to have them for all the students, and those who had low expectations tended to have them for all the students. In her research, she tested the students after a month in their new class, gave the teachers the results, and then asked them to predict the student's attainment at the end of the year. Sure enough, those teachers who had high expectations were more likely to enhance their students' learning, and those who had low expectations had hardly changed the students' growth over a year.

In another study, Rubie-Davies (2014) showed that when teachers who believed indigenous groups (in her case, Maori students) were typically lower, this affected (negatively) the performance of these students – and this was despite the finding that Maori students' performance was not below that of any other ethnic group at the beginning of the year. This can lead to these students becoming aware of the teacher's expectations and then performing in line with them. Rubie-Davies (2014) observed that teachers with high expectations engage in a number of practices well supported by effective teaching literature that distinguished them from low expectations teachers. The high expectations teachers are more likely to connect new concepts with prior knowledge, use scaffolding techniques to support learning, provide more frequent and high-quality feedback, question frequently, and have a greater use of open-ended questioning.

Thus, a key part of this mindframe is whether teachers have high or low (or worse, zero) expectations for all their students. The climate of the class, the perception by the students about the foundations of the relationships with their teachers can communicate expectations – which then can be translated into actions for good or bad. One of the major claims of the Visible Learning work is that the differences in these expectations help account for a large part of the variance among teachers in their effectiveness. Given that students experience and come to believe the teachers' expectations, it can be seen how important it is that teachers work collaboratively within and across schools to calibrate their expectations – what does it mean to be "good at" history, music, panel beating; what does it mean to say this represents "a year's growth"?

Teacher–student relationships

It has long been known that one of the most fundamental insights from educational research is that a positive teacher-student relationship is essential for successful learning. It may be seen as a sine qua non of school learning, and so it comes as no surprise that this factor achieves an effect size of 0.72 in Visible Learning (see Figure 9.2). The significance of teacher-student relationships is beyond dispute, yet maintaining these relationships is a complex task: Teachers need to possess a number of skills to create a learning-conducive atmosphere, and this relates to positive relations not only between the students and teacher but also among the students. Although there is a great variety of research on teacher-student relationships, the example of parenting styles may serve to illustrate the main messages. It is common to distinguish between four parenting styles

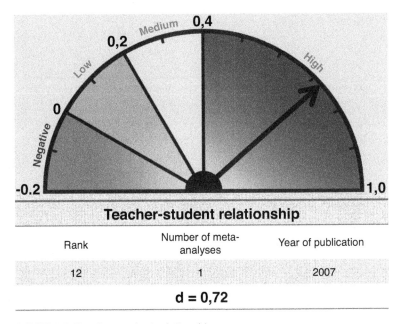

Teacher-student relationship

Rank	Number of meta-analyses	Year of publication
12	1	2007

d = 0,72

FIGURE 9.2 Teacher-student relationship

Source: Hattie and Zierer (2017).

that vary in their effectiveness at fostering personality development: authoritarian, indulgent, neglectful, and authoritative. They differ essentially about their relative positions along the dimensions of closeness vs. distance and control vs. freedom. The authoritarian parenting style is characterized by a low degree of closeness and a high degree of control. The permissive parenting style, on the other hand, is marked by a high degree of closeness and a low degree of control. The neglectful parenting style involves a low degree of both closeness and control. Finally, the authoritative parenting style involves a high degree of both closeness and control. Although the assessment of these typologies is not always identical in the literature, there is general agreement on the point that an authoritative parenting style has the greatest potential for effective learning. Such a style creates a sense of fairness, predictability, and thus safety to be engaged in learning, with all the related notions of making errors, seeking help, and working positively with others. This creates optimal conditions for students to be prepared to feel safe in making errors, stretching themselves into discovering new relations behind ideas, and learning from their errors.

Reducing anxiety

A little anxiety can help; a lot of anxiety can be a major barrier. In these latter circumstances, we typically fight (actively resist, be naughty, create a distraction or disturbance) or flight (not participate, resist engaging, or show boredom). Consequently, methods for reducing levels of anxiety (and thus avoiding fight or flight) have a positive effect on learning processes and achieve an effect size of 0.40 in Visible Learning (see Figure 9.3). We also note that boredom wins the prize as the lowest or most negative influence (d = −.49). This implies that teachers should avoid approaches that cause undue anxiety in their students and instead choose approaches that reduce their anxiety and engage them in the challenges or learning and inspire confidence and trust. What this will benefit above all is the learners' self-efficacy, another factor with an effect size (d = 0.47) in the zone of desired effects, because students will then approach challenges with more confidence. It is getting this balance right between no challenge and too much challenge that is the zone of learning. Similarly, in this zone, there is sufficient angst but not too much to turn the student off from attempting the task (the fight or flight).

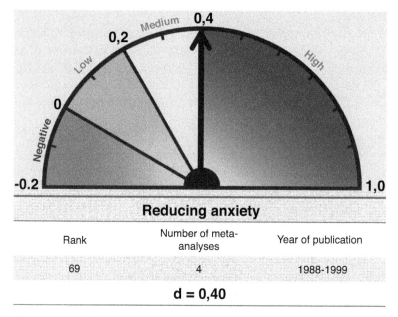

Rank	Number of meta-analyses	Year of publication
69	4	1988-1999

d = 0,40

FIGURE 9.3 Reducing anxiety

Source: Hattie and Zierer (2017).

In this zone, students will no longer attribute their achievement to their abilities but to the effort they put into the task. The key is that building these positive relations between teachers and students and between the students is that it creates the conditions where it is OK to make mistakes in front of others, to actively explore other ideas and critique them, and to learn from others.

As mentioned earlier, the empirical evidence in support of the mindframe "I build relationships and trust so that learning can occur in a place where it is safe to make mistakes and learn from others" can serve as a basis for concrete guidelines that are suitable for immediate implementation in the classroom. We present several examples in the following.

The IKEA effect

Are you familiar with the IKEA effect (cf. Hattie & Yates, 2015, p. 295; Norton, Mochon, & Airely, 2012)? Even if you are not, you certainly know IKEA and have perhaps also found that it is not so easy to assemble a bookshelf out of the thousands of parts you get when you buy a flat pack. Studies on consumer psychology have determined that people who succeed in doing it value the IKEA bookshelf more highly than an expensive piece of antique furniture. This is because we have higher value for things we are involved in creating or solving – it is a product of all the effort and hard work it took to put the bookshelf together. This effort and this hard work pass seemingly directly into the product, remain fixed in our memory, and lead to an increase in value. What implications does this suggest for school and instruction? Whenever a learner puts in effort and hard work to complete an assignment, it is the teacher's duty to show the learner respect and admiration for his or her achievement. Teachers who do so strengthen the teacher–student relationship; those who do not jeopardize the teacher–student relationship.

Not "not" but "not yet"

It is one of the simplest study designs in psychology research, and even more astounding are the results: The purpose of Carol Dweck's (2012) study, which has since become known under the simple phrase "not yet," was to determine what difference it makes whether teachers tell their students "You can't do it" or "You can't do it yet." Whereas the former statement demotivates, frustrates, and stigmatizes the learners, the latter statement makes them more confident and willing to make an effort and thus leads to better performance. Why? Because this "not yet" signals to the learners that they can achieve the goal if they put in effort, that they are on the right track and that it is worth it to carry on in the same vein, and that their hard work has a chance of being crowned with success if they keep working to improve themselves. This implies that it is very important for teachers to always carefully consider their own language in the classroom, especially in giving their students feedback, and to reflect on it with a colleague.

Send out a smile

The idea that humor and cheerfulness are an essential part of successful instruction and have a positive influence on the learning process is nothing new. We can find statements to this effect going all the way back to ancient times. Now we also have empirical findings to back up these statements and demonstrate that instruction can best succeed with humor and cheerfulness. This does not mean that teachers should make their students laugh all the time, let alone turn themselves into clowns. The correlations of using humor in workplaces in general is substantial ($r = .36$ with work performance, $.29$ with coping effectiveness, $.21$ with health, $-.23$ with burnout, and $-.20$ with stress; cf. Mesmer-Magnus, Glew, & Viswesvaran, 2012). As serious a matter as learning is, however, it also needs to include phases that give everyone involved a chance to laugh about themselves, about the subject, and about school. Humor can take the pressure off being at the edge of our abilities, making mistakes, and not knowing where next to go. Psychologically speaking, teachers always have a trump card they can play, because a smile is contagious – especially when it comes from the heart, is sincere and authentic, and is shared in a community. A study on this phenomenon was conducted in the 1990s (cf. Hattie & Yates, 2015, p. 250): The researchers smiled at strangers in the pedestrian zones of large cities, and more than half of them smiled back instinctively. It is, therefore, our job as teachers to make our students laugh and to make sure humor and cheerfulness have a place in our classrooms. Just as a smile sends out positive signals about relationship building, a failure to smile sends out negative signals. Teachers who walk into the classroom grumpy should not be surprised that their students never laugh and are more inclined to be grumpy also – unless it is to laugh at them behind their backs for being such a grump. There is every reason to make learning fun and joyful, especially when the learning is challenging.

The chameleon effect and the power of rules and rituals

Rules and rituals are part of every community and a distinguishing feature of cultures. They provide orientation, inspire confidence and trust, create a feeling of belonging and community, and are an expression of mutual esteem. It is thus worth the trouble to make up a list of rules and rituals for the classroom as a common and consistent basis for strengthening teacher-student relationships. It can and should include simple things, like the ritual of beginning class each day with a greeting and concluding with a dismissal, or the ritual of ending class each day with exit tickets to celebrate the day's learning. They can be requested at the end of the lesson to document learning, to evaluate the effectiveness of the learning, or to emphasize processes of learning (Fisher, Frey & Farnan, 2004).

Interesting in this regard are the studies on the so-called chameleon effect. They demonstrate that we unintentionally change our behavior to match that of others we interact with in our social environment, including our posture, casual movements, gestures, facial expressions, and speech tempo, to name but a few examples. This effect can already be observed in young children imitating their parents, but it is also found in offices as well as in schools and classrooms. For example, if teachers ask lots of questions that everyone knows they already know the answer to, then often students ask teachers questions they tend to already know the answer to – questioning becomes a performance rather than an inquiry. The chameleon effect illustrates that people interact unconsciously with those around them and adjust their behavior to match each other. This process is also known as mimicry and has been explained in neuroscientific terms in the mirror neuron theory (cf. Hattie & Yates, 2015, p. 278). The more intense our relationships are, the more closely we imitate each other.

The implications of these findings for school and instruction are self-evident: Teachers can serve as role models by being passionate, and by bringing our competence and mindframes to bear, we can get our students to adopt similar mindframes. So teachers need to pay attention to how they enter the classroom, how they interact with learners, how they react when they make a mistake, and what gestures and facial expressions they use. Have someone watch for these cues while you are teaching or, better, watch what your students do and ask "are they copying my own behaviors?"

In one of the most powerful theories explaining change, the theory of reasoned action (Fishbein & Ajzen, 1975), subjective norms are among the most important predictors of change. Subjective norms are related to the perceived social pressure to engage or not to engage in a behavior (like ceasing smoking, having a body image, working hard at a task). Therefore, the rules and rituals that you establish in your class (or school) are so important. Learners who follow rules and rituals have a positive influence on their peers.

The opposite case, namely teachers or learners with negative behaviors, can have a negative effect on their peers. Disruptive behavior can be contagious and make other learners in the class into troublemakers. The studies on classroom management referred to in Chapter 4, "I am a change agent and believe all students can improve" call attention to this point and stress the importance of getting such behavior under control as soon as possible to avoid negative consequences – such negative behavior cannot become a "subjective norm." Talk with the disruptive learner and take on this challenge to change the behavior of disruptive behavior. Only with this mindframe can you be successful.

Once a liar, always a liar: credibility as the core of an intact teacher-student relationship

In most situations, a lack of credibility in a leader makes human co-existence extremely difficult. It, therefore, comes as no surprise that the factor "teacher credibility" achieves an effect size of 0.90 in Visible Learning.

How can a learner identify whether a teacher is credible? Most students would say that credible teachers are fair in their judgments. We saw earlier the importance of a sense of fairness, and this is often a more desired attribute in a teacher than many other attributes (such as whether they are tough, friendly, laissez-faire). Other students would say credible teachers are sincere. We also saw earlier the importance of sincerity in our discussion of the IKEA effect and Carol Dweck's "not yet" study. This means taking students and their work seriously and giving them the attention they are due, keeping learning paths open by avoiding superficial feedback, and working with students to help them progress to the desired success criteria of lessons. Similarly, it means not playing down the significance of mistakes or ignoring them altogether. This is not the way to gain the trust of learners – particularly those who are aware of what they do not know (yet). The qualities that are called for here, and the qualities that provide the key to strengthening the teacher-student relationship, are the competence and the mindframe to provide the learner differentiated feedback.

Where can I start?

The examples described in this chapter underline the influence teachers can have in regard to the crucial factor of relationships in the classroom. Keep the following aspects in mind: your general demeanor, your posture, your gestures and facial expressions, your tone of voice, your smile, and your eye contact. It is important not only *what* teachers say in the classroom, but also *how* and *why* they say it. It is, therefore, important to consider again and again, particularly in difficult situations, what you say and *how* and *why* you say it. Question yourself and observe your effects on the learners. Use the possibilities of new media and make a video recording of yourself teaching ("micro-teaching," which also includes making videos, achieves an effect size of 0.88) – this is fast and easy to do with smartphones. However, it is not enough to just record a video. You also need to analyze it and interpret it. Talk with the learners and your colleagues to obtain an outside perspective. Questions like "What do I expect?" "What is encouraging?" "What surprises me?" and "What do I want to change?" can provide a basis for such reflection.

The ideas presented in this chapter show how closely the mindframe "I build relationships and trust so that learning can occur in a place where it is safe to make mistakes and learn from others" relates to the other mindframes discussed in this book. Here are just two quick examples: First, "I focus on learning and the language of learning" requires a learning culture in which mistakes are welcome and are a necessary part of the learning process, and this is not possible without intact teacher-student relationships. Second, "I give and help students understand feedback and I interpret and act on feedback given to me" illustrates the great complexity of the interaction between the learners and the teacher and shows how teacher-student relationships can be strengthened through feedback. Hence, it is especially important here to keep the other chapters in this book in mind.

As with many of the mindframes, developing positive relationships is a means to an end – it forms a resource to be spent when in challenging situations. When students do not know what to do next, when they make mistakes, or when they are confused, the power of the trust developed by the teacher and among peers can then really pay off. When there are strong positive relationships, no one will respond to a student making a mistake by saying, "there goes stupid again" or laugh or smirk at errors. The positive relations lead to the trust to engage in challenge, to have a try at a difficult task, to build the confidence to engage in hard work.

CHECKLIST

Reflect on the following points next time you plan a lesson:

- Take stock of the expectations you have for your students.
- Avoid negative attributions.
- Try to keep an open and positive attitude toward the learning processes of your students.
- Keep in mind that everyone is capable of learning, even in situations that seem hopeless.
- Whenever you see that your students are trying, show your appreciation for their work and achievements.
- Consider your language and use expressions that signal to the learners that they can achieve the goal if they try. "Not yet" is better than "not."
- Allow room for humor and cheerfulness in your class and laugh with your students.
- Be a role model and make use of the chameleon effect.
- Make sure you remain credible in your behavior. Be honest and fair by explaining the reasons for your decisions.

EXERCISES

- Go back to the questionnaire for self-reflection at the start of the chapter and complete it again in another color. Where and, more important, why has your perspective on the statements changed? Discuss your self-assessment with a colleague.

- Plan your next lesson and include a phase designed to show your appreciation for your students' achievements. Consult the checklist in planning this phase. Discuss your plan and the lesson with a colleague.

- Laugh or make a humorous comment about school or instruction in one of your next lessons and try to determine what effect it has on the learners. Reflect on your experience with a colleague.

I focus on learning and the language of learning

QUESTIONNAIRE FOR SELF-REFLECTION

Assess yourself by rating your agreement with the following statements: 1 = strongly disagree, 5 = strongly agree

I am very good at . . .

identifying the strengths and weaknesses of my students.

determining what prior academic knowledge my students have.

I know perfectly well . . .

that my students' prior experiences need to be taken into account.

what achievement level my students are at.

My goal is always to . . .

take into account the strengths and weaknesses of my students.

take into account the prior academic knowledge of my students when teaching.

I am thoroughly convinced . . .

that it is important to know the strengths and weaknesses of my students.

that I should take into account the prior academic knowledge of my students when teaching.

VIGNETTE

From the life of a first grader: Victoria likes going to school. She wants to learn reading, writing, and arithmetic. She went to preschool for a long time and did a lot of tracing, coloring, and counting to prepare herself for learning these skills. And now it's her first day at school. She's finally with the big kids. And what does she have to do in the first weeks? Trace, color, and count. She asks the teacher why she has to do the same things she did in preschool all over again. She's not convinced by the answer she receives: "Because we all start from scratch."

What is this chapter about?

This vignette illustrates this chapter's main message: We do not start from scratch when we learn something. We come to the learning with prior skills, will, and a sense of thrill for learning. Learning is an active and self-directed process – but success lies not only the learner: Much also lies in the hands of the teachers, and they can decide whether the learner has the potential to take on the learning alone, with others, or with much expert assistance. Knowledge of the students' initial learning level and a willingness to take it as a starting point for instructional thought and action may be seen in this connection as prerequisites for successful teaching, and consequently also for successful learning.

When you finish reading this chapter, you should be able to take this message as a basis for explaining:

- how significant the factors "Piagetian programs," "prior achievement," "personality," and "concept mapping" are.
- why we should stick to the term "teacher."
- what the dumb-and-dumber effect is and how to deal with it.
- what the mindframe "I focus on learning and the language of learning has to do with the "invisible gorilla" studies.
- what aspects of cognitive load theory are important for this mindframe.

- why it is not very useful to talk about learning styles.

- what self-concept involves and what significance it has for successful learning.

Which factors from Visible Learning support this mindframe?

The advice that one should start with learning rather than with teaching has become a well-known dictum at least since the cognitive turn in psychology. But what this actually entails is less clear. Most teachers agree with this principle, but they are also often uncertain what it means concretely for their teaching.

Perhaps it would be helpful to take a historical perspective and start from the beginning. In the previous century, theories of teaching and learning were long dominated by *behaviorism*. The main idea of this approach is that learning always happens when one sends out the right stimuli, which then becomes the task of teaching. This idea was derived from numerous experiments with animals, one of the most famous of which was Pavlov's dog. Ivan Pavlov demonstrated in an experiment that he could make the saliva that collects in a dog's mouth when it sees food also collect there when it hears a bell. He had previously conditioned the dog over an extended time period by ringing a bell each time he showed it food – critics of the approach have since maintained that they have also observed this phenomenon in students after the recess bell has rung. The main objection to behaviorism is that it fails to take account of the cognitive processes that take place during learning. This is due not least to the limitations in the methodological approach common in the heyday of behaviorism: It turns learning into a passive process. What matters from a behaviorist perspective is essentially the external stimuli. All the teacher needs to do is choose the right stimuli to make learning happen. Methods like learning from models thus play a special role in behaviorism – and we should not forget how much we learn every day of our lives in exactly this way.

Researchers then began concentrating their efforts more strongly on what is happening in this "black box" and designing experiments aimed at figuring out what happens in the heads of the learners – *cognitivism* was born. Jean Piaget conducted groundbreaking studies in this paradigm, most of them based on observations of experiments with his children. Piaget established that stimuli can lead to various reactions and that these reactions depend on cognitive structures that develop over time: The learner either assimilates the stimuli by attempting to bring them into line with his or her existing cognitive structures or accommodates the existing structures by attempting to bring them in line with the stimuli. When the new stimuli led to disagreements with currently held ideas this led to disequilibrium – which is a major moment for successful learning to occur. This makes learning into an active process based predominantly on information processing. Consequently, the teacher needs to have knowledge of the learners' existing cognitive structures in order to influence them.

The work started by the cognitivists was further intensified in the next movement, *constructivism*. This is not the place to trace the development of constructivism in detail. In the following, we touch only on several core aspects of the theory that are necessary for understanding the mindframe "I focus on learning and the language of learning": Constructivism makes an even more concentrated effort than cognitivism to gain access to the black box and determine what happens when people learn. However, in many cases, it proves impossible to predict how people take in and process information. As an illustration, consider this prominent example from Paul Watzlawick. He asks: Who is right, the pessimist who says the glass is half empty, or the optimist who says the glass is half full? There are different realities. Nevertheless, constructivism stresses that learning is an active process that can be controlled by the individual, and this means that here, too, teachers need to be aware of their students' initial learning level in order to react adequately to their needs.

As this quick overview demonstrates, there are different teaching and learning theories that cast the learners and teachers in various roles. The current discourse often leaves the impression that constructivism must be right because it comes last in the historical sequence of teaching and learning theories. However, cognitivism and even behaviorism remain significant teaching and learning theories today. This is clear even just from the fact touched upon earlier that people learn a lot from models as children and even into adulthood. Ultimately, the important thing is to organize the various teaching and learning theories into a coherent system. Identifying the different ways in which these theories regard making mistakes plays an important part in this endeavor: Whereas behaviorism has the goal of preventing mistakes, cognitivism and constructivism view mistakes as necessary or even desirable. Learning means making mistakes, and mistakes make learning visible.

The results of Visible Learning should also be seen and interpreted against the backdrop of these developments in teaching and learning theories. A number of factors illustrate what is meant by the mind-frame "I focus on learning and the language of learning."

Piagetian programs

The factor "Piagetian programs" achieves an effect size of d = 1.28, one of the highest effects in Visible Learning (see Figure 10.1). Among the many contributions made by Jean Piaget is the idea that children change in the ways they think and process as they grow. Their thinking develops qualitatively through successive stages under the influence of maturation and of the social and physical environment. He described four stages: Sensorimotor, Pre-Operational, Concrete Operational, and the Formal Operation stages. In the first stage (about 0–2 years), the child exhibits a completely egocentric approach to the world, is unable to separate thoughts from action, and is unable to recognize that the perspective of the object would differ depending on their position relative to object. The child then moves to the Pre-Operational stage from ages 2 to 7 years, where object

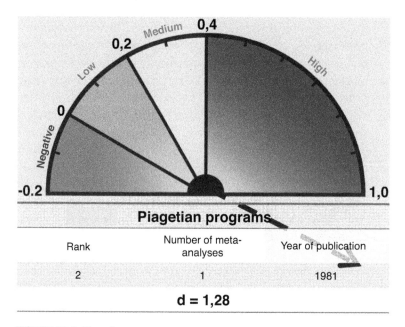

FIGURE 10.1 Piagetian programs

Source: Hattie and Zierer (2017).

permanence is firmly established and symbolic thoughts develop. To move to the next stage, referred to as the Concrete Operational stage (7–11 years), a child needs to be able to perform what Piaget called Operations, which are internalized actions that the individual can use to manipulate, transform, and then return an object to its original state. The child understands the principle of conservation, which states that the quantity of an object can be determined to be the same despite a change in shape or volume of a container. This stage is also marked by the child beginning to apply logic to steps and stages, assessed through the A not B task in which an object is hidden from the child in one of two different locations. The final stage from 11 to 16 years, the Formal Operation stage, is characterized by abstract and hypothetical thought.

It is important to recall that Piaget argued the movement across stages occurred via disequilibrium. That is, they began to realize that what they were doing, thinking, and trying to accommodate into their current thinking was discrepant – hence again the mindframe about privileging errors and misunderstandings. They are the essence of growth. Bolton and Hattie (in review) have mapped the physical changes in the brain and the development of self-regulation between 0–20, and the major changes in how we self-regulate are almost perfectly related to these four Piagetian stages. Self-regulation relates to the ability to inhibit distractions, updating and monitor one's working memory representations, and shifting between tasks or mental sets.

We are not suggesting a matching process, where teaching is focused on supporting the current thinking of the child (and, indeed, it is hard to much evidence for such matching [Adey & Shayer, 2013]), but there is much support for programs that maximize the rate of cognitive development of every child. Shayer and Adey (1981) developed, for example, a series of Cognitive Acceleration projects based on the assumption that cognitive development can be accelerated. The model is based on three big ideas. First, the mind develops in response to challenge, or to disequilibrium, so the intervention must provide some cognitive conflict. Second, the mind has a growing ability to become conscious of and so take control of its own processes, so the intervention must encourage students to be metacognitive. Third, cognitive development is a social process promoted by high-quality discussion among peers that are deliberately structured. Their programs had remarkable success, focused on learning and how it is developed, and are well worth further investigation (Adey, Shayer, & Yates, 2001; Shayer & Adey, 1993; Shayer, 1999).

Prior achievement

The factor "prior achievement" points in a similar direction, with a similarly high effect size of 0.65 in Visible Learning (see Figure 10.2). The studies in question investigated issues like the significance of prior academic success for continued success in the future. It should not come as a surprise that the predictions made on the basis of prior achievement are generally highly accurate. A study that has become particularly well known in this context is the marshmallow experiment conducted by Walter Mischel in the 1970s. It involved a task in which preschool children were given the choice of waiting in a room for 15 minutes to receive a desirable reward, such as two marshmallows, or ending the wait at any time and accepting a less desirable reward, such as only a single marshmallow (cf. Mischel, 2014; for a discussion, cf. Hattie & Yates, 2015, p. 234). Only very few preschool children were capable of waiting – and those who were turned out in longitudinal studies to be more successful in their subsequent educational and career paths. The conclusion that is still often drawn from this study today is that some people are more successful from their

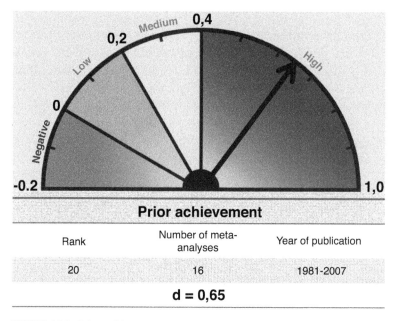

Rank	Number of meta-analyses	Year of publication
20	16	1981-2007

d = 0,65

FIGURE 10.2 Prior achievement

Source: Hattie and Zierer (2017).

socialization in their early years and that many of the things that make up success are already fixed in early childhood. This interpretation is false and misconceives the main idea behind the marshmallow experiment and the mindframe "I focus on learning and the language of learning." First of all, the result does not support the assumption, quite common up to the time the study was conducted, that the ability to resist temptation to obtain a more valuable reward leads to success. Instead, it demonstrates the effectiveness of a different ability: After the task had been assigned, it could be observed how some of the preschool children began diverting their attention – whether consciously or unconsciously – away from the marshmallow as a sweet reward they could enjoy at any time and toward the toy airplane, car, or ship they were playing with.

The time flew by as the children played, and 15 minutes later, they received their two marshmallows. This encapsulates the main idea of the mindframe "I focus on learning and the language of learning." People differ in regard to not only their knowledge and ability but also their will and judgment, their wishes, their interests, and their needs, and hence also in regard to their ability to focus their attention. The implication is not that people with the best talents are always the most successful, but that it is the job of teachers to provide their students the support they need to cope with the challenges of life. This was easy to do in the marshmallow experiment: Even just telling the children to think of the marshmallow as an airplane, car, or ship was often enough to help them wait longer for their reward. While prior achievement is doubtlessly an influential factor for learning, it is by no means a dogma – although it can become one if the teacher draws the wrong conclusions from it. It should be kept in mind but not simply accepted as a natural fact.

Personality

Although the factor "personality" achieves an effect size only of 0.18 in Visible Learning, it is still significant for visible learning and successful teaching (see Figure 10.3). This is primarily because "personality" encapsulated so much, and there are specific dispositions that are more critical. It is now common to see five major factors, "the big five," as the major dimensions of personality:

- *neuroticism* or the capacity to cope with negative emotions
- *extraversion* or the capacity to engage in interpersonal interactions

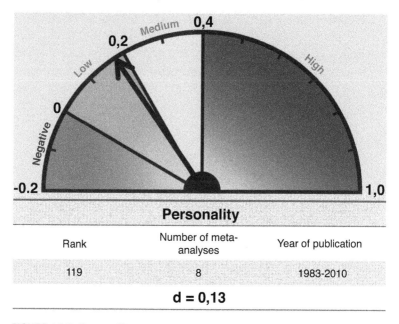

Personality

Rank	Number of meta-analyses	Year of publication
119	8	1983-2010

d = 0,13

FIGURE 10.3 Personality

Source: Hattie and Zierer (2017).

- *openness to experience* or the capacity to seek out new experiences
- *conscientiousness* or the capacity to act in a controlled, purposeful, and precise manner
- *agreeableness* or the capacity to be cooperative and empathetic.

Although the big five can have predictive power in many contexts, they are less significant in regard to successful learning – with one important exception: conscientiousness. This appears to be one of the key traits for learners on the path to academic success. Against this backdrop, one of the main tasks of the teacher in enabling learning is to observe the way students work in general and their conscientiousness in particular.

There is a popular trend to consider conscientiousness as "grit" (which can also include perseverance). As with all personality variables, it is incorrect to overgeneralize and say a person has "grit" or "conscientiousness," as it depends on the task and situation. The main time we would want to see this skill being used is in situations of tension, when the student makes a mistake, to continue on the task if there is a reasonable probability of still getting it correct, and when overlearning is a desirable exercise. We do not want to develop "grit" and run courses on "grit," as we want to develop this skill to be able to be applied at the right time to the right ends. It is knowing when to be conscientious and to what ends that is more important.

Concept mapping

There are many methods for taking account of the learners and their initial learning level in the process of lesson planning. They all have high effect sizes. To take just one example, the factor "concept mapping" has an effect size of 0.60 in Visible Learning (see Figure 10.4) – provided we develop or co-construct concept maps with students (not merely give them one). What this method involves is essentially summarizing and structuring students' knowledge in a particular field of knowledge. This gives students information on what has worked in the past and how they can shape and support their learning process in the future. The results of the meta-analyses on this factor indicate that concept mapping is most effective after initial exposure to

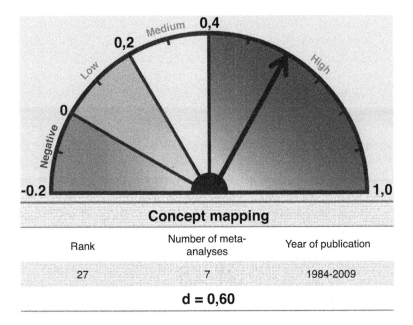

Concept mapping

Rank	Number of meta-analyses	Year of publication
27	7	1984-2009

d = 0,60

FIGURE 10.4 Concept mapping

Source: Hattie and Zierer (2017).

a new topic. In pedagogical terms, it is, therefore, located close to surface understanding and at the transition to deep understanding. This means that taking stock of prior knowledge and experiences is important not just at the beginning of a new teaching sequence but is something that needs to be done continuously throughout the learning process. "I focus on learning and the language of learning" is thus a mindframe that is significant for every learner, from the novice to the expert.

Learning facilitator, learning coach, learning counselor? No, *teacher*

In retrospect, it comes as little surprise that many educators were full of enthusiasm for the paradigm shift initiated by constructivism. Many took this change in the perception of learning as an occasion to come up with words to describe the teacher's new role in the classroom. "Learning facilitator" and "learning coach" are just a few of the suggestions raised in this context. The problem is that the teacher begins to consider their role as standing alongside the student (the guide on the side) rather than feeding back and feeding forward. When students are being challenged, they often experience the edge of their understanding, revel in challenges and thus need expertise to move forward (into Vygotsky's zone of proximal development, where he claimed he would never venture without support).

The dumb-and-dumber effect

David Dunning and Justin Kruger, after whom the dumb-and-dumber effect is also called the Dunning-Kruger effect, conducted an experiment in which they asked a group of college students to estimate their scores on a test after leaving the examination room (cf. Hattie & Yates, 2015, p. 224). It turned out that the low-achieving students overestimated their score by up to 20 percent, whereas the top-achieving students underestimated it by up to 5 percent. Putting it bluntly, we might conclude: Incompetent people are unable to assess their own incompetence. Alternatively, we might frame it in Socratic terms and say from the perspective of the competent people: I know that I know nothing.

For school contexts, what this result suggests is that learners are not always capable of accurately assessing themselves and their performance. As a consequence, the teacher needs to remain present in the background and intervene if necessary whenever the learners are expected to make such assessments. This connection of open learning environments is designed with many different stages targeting various achievement levels. Once the teacher has explained the stages of such environments to the learners, it is generally up to them to choose the ones they think are right for them. However, the dumb-and-dumber effect warns that this way of going about things will not necessarily go off as intended. Low-achieving students will often choose tasks that are too difficult, whereas high-achieving students will be liable to choose tasks that are too easy. Hence, even in an open learning environment, it is the competence and mindframes of the teacher that decide whether learning succeeds. It is challenging the student on the basis of where they are currently to where they need to be. This is another reason why we need to develop assessment capable students so they are more able to know in reliable ways their current performance (and not overestimate or underestimate).

The "invisible gorilla" study

An experiment conducted by Christopher Chabris and Daniel Simons provides a similar example of what can happen when one places excessive demands on learners. Videos of several versions of the experiment may be found at theinvisiblegorilla.com/ or on YouTube (cf. Hattie & Yates, 2015, p. 271). Students are shown a video in which two groups of basketball players, dressed in black and white T-shirts, pass balls back and forth. The task of the students is to count the passes made by the team in the white shirts. Several seconds into the video, a person in a gorilla suit appears at the right edge of the screen and walks across the court, stopping briefly in the middle and then walking off again to the left.

Astoundingly, only slightly more than 40 percent of test subjects see the gorilla. For the rest, the gorilla remains invisible. The explanation for this phenomenon lies in the fact that the test subjects are under a high level of mental load because they are so focused on the task of counting the passes, and this leads them to overlook many other aspects of the scene.

The implication for school and instruction is that it is important to keep in mind the students' initial learning level and to check whether the pedagogical design of learning process leads to an unnecessary load. Hence, here as well the goal is to make learning the focal point of teaching. Sometimes we become so preoccupied in the task we forget where we are meant to be going, and we may see aids to help us complete tasks.

The cognitive load theory and its implications for instruction

What happens when learners choose tasks that are too difficult or when the learning environment is not designed appropriately? In other words, what happens when the level of mental strain becomes too high for the learners? These are questions addressed by cognitive load theory, which was developed by Paul Chandler and John Sweller (cf. Kiel et al., 2014, p. 86). They take the lead from cognitivism and Piaget in assuming that learning processes generate new schemas that are linked to existing schemas. This always involves the presence of three types of cognitive load on the working memory: intrinsic, extraneous, and germane.

First, intrinsic load has to do with the difficulty of the tasks and the achievement level of the students. The more difficult the task is, the greater the intrinsic load will be. This means that the learner's prior experience and knowledge are very important. Second, extraneous load depends on the presentation and design of the learning environment in general and the learning material in particular. For example, if the learning material is full of unnecessary information, is presented in a confusing way, and is strewn with a glut of cross-references, the cognitive load will be higher in this area. Third, germane cognitive load results from the effort to understand the learning material and thus acquire knowledge. The connection between this type of cognitive load and the first two is evident: The higher the intrinsic and extraneous load is, the higher the germane load will be. These considerations suggest the conclusion that instruction should aim to keep the extraneous load as low as possible to reserve as much load as possible for schema generation and knowledge acquisition.

Cognitive overload may thus have various causes, and it stems essentially from two sources: First, it may arise from being overwhelmed by factors like an inaccurate self-assessment, a situation already touched upon in our discussion of the dumb-and-dumber effect. The type of load that needs to be adjusted in this case is intrinsic load. Second, it may arise from being overwhelmed by an overuse of methodology, for instance worksheets that are so crammed with teaching tools that they end up concealing the learning goal and the learning content and relegating them to the background. Primary school mathematics lessons, for instance, can become muddled with a proliferation of arithmetic trees, arithmetic triangles, and arithmetic wheels. Although the use of such innovations does bespeak a certain pedagogical creativity, they often place unnecessary strain on their intended audience and are, therefore, not better than classical methods. The type of load that needs to be adjusted in this case is extraneous load, and the invisible gorilla is a popular example of this type of overload.

Learning styles: a myth of empirical educational research

It is one of the most frequent claims we read in our students' research papers, and we stumble upon it even occasionally in the literature: Learners retain 10 percent of what they read, 20 percent of what they hear, 30 percent of what they see, 50 percent of what they see and hear, 70 percent of what they present themselves, and 90 percent of what they do themselves. These figures might sound plausible at first, but they have no basis at all in empirical findings: Not a single study provides evidence for them. And if we take a closer look, we will be forced to admit that it is not even conceivable that a study could produce such clear evidence. Even just the obvious objection that it must also depend on what learners read, what they hear, what they see, what they see and hear, and what they present and do themselves should make us skeptical of this claim.

All the same, there is (or was) a long-established tradition in empirical educational research that attempts to produce these or similar learning retention figures – in retrospect, one might say that the temptation of revolutionizing learning, or perhaps also the prospect of making a lot of money, was evidently too great.

Accordingly, the factor "matching style of learning" originally achieved a high average effect size of 0.41 in Visible Learning. However, the discussion of this factor in *Visible Learning* already raised objections to several of the studies included in this result, and this led in *Visible Learning for Teachers* to a correction of the data and the exclusion of three meta-analyses. The result is a much lower effect size of 0.17. This is a clear case where quality of studies (implausible effect sizes, tiny samples, and statistical errors) reduces what seems like a reasonable effect to close to the zero point. What is the reason for this skepticism about learning styles, and what arguments can be put forward against the belief in learning styles?

There is no justification for classifying students according to some beliefs about how they think. There is, however, much justification for teachers using multiple ways of engaging students' thinking strategies in their teaching. We do not have but one or even a dominant way of thinking, and the most successful students are more adept at choosing appropriate learning strategies depending on where they are in the learning cycle – they have many and are adaptive in choosing or changing them depending on the situation (Hattie & Donoghue, 2016).

If we wish to wrest an overall message from this research tradition, we might say the following: Learning is effective to the extent that it is enjoyable, and the best way to make it enjoyable is not by ensuring that particular conditions have been met but by designing a learning situation that takes up the thread of the learners' prior knowledge and experiences, ties in with their existing thinking, and thereby presents them with a challenge. In a nutshell, when we learn there can be a joyful emotion from this success – so learning breeds joy. Engagement typically follows, not necessarily precedes, success in learning.

Self-concept: a key to successful learning

A chapter about the mindframe "I focus on learning and the language of learning" would not be complete without a discussion of one of the most influential factors of successful learning: self-concept. It allows us to illustrate what it means to take the prior knowledge and experiences of the learners as the starting point for teaching.

This factor has an effect size of 0.47 in Visible Learning. What is meant by self-concept? An analogy often used to answer this question is the rope model (see Figure 10.5; cf. Hattie, 1992).

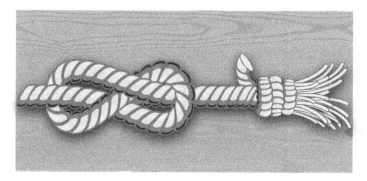

FIGURE 10.5 Rope

The rope model emphasizes that our self-concept consists not in a single fiber but many overlapping self-concepts and that the strength of the rope does not depend on any one fiber extending throughout the length of the rope but on many intertwining fibers. These many fibers refer to the processes of self-concept. In the following, we will go into two of these processes in more detail by way of illustration: self-efficacy and motivation.

In regard to self-efficacy, there are some learners who tend to attribute their successes to luck and put their failures down to deficiencies in their personalities, which has a negative impact on their self-concept. There are other learners who tend to attribute their successes to effort and attempt to explain their failures by telling themselves they need to put in more effort next time. Whereas the first group of learners has low self-efficacy beliefs, the second group of learners has high self-efficacy beliefs. Learners with high self-efficacy beliefs have better chances than those with low self-efficacy beliefs of being successful in the long term, because they seek challenges, put in effort, and are enthusiastic about learning. Perhaps even more important, they regard mistakes as an opportunity.

Differences in motivation have a similar effect on learning: There are some learners who learn because they expect to earn a reward (extrinsic motivation), and there are other learners who learn because they are interested in the material (intrinsic motivation). As many people expect to be the case and know from personal experience, differences in motivation do not show themselves in a willingness to perform. Rather, they show themselves in long-term learning gains on one hand and depth of understanding on the other. In both cases, intrinsic motivation is superior to extrinsic motivation.

Accordingly, teachers need to know how their students process information relating to their own person. This enables them to develop and improve their confidence in being able to complete challenging tasks, their persistence in the face of mistakes and failures, their openness and willingness to interact with peers, and their pride in investing energy in activities that lead to successful learning. Before engaging students in learning, it is, therefore, important not just to take stock of their prior knowledge and experiences but also to conduct a thorough analysis of their self-concept.

Where can I start?

Keeping tabs on the initial learning levels of students at all times is doubtlessly one of the greatest challenges teachers are confronted with in everyday school life: It is difficult, time-consuming, and often does not even lead to any new insight. And yet it is an important ingredient in the task of taking learning as the starting point for teaching. What do they bring to the task in terms of their skill, will, and sense of thrill? What is the criteria of success that is desired over the term of the learning? How are they going from where they are to where we would like them to be?

In light of the ideas presented in this chapter, a number of questions seem important. For instance, there seems to be no use in analyzing learning styles because there is little evidence that they are an influential factor for learning. On the other hand, it seems essential to take a close look at the nature of how students are learning, in particular, school subjects: Is the learner still thinking concretely, or can he or she manipulate ideas and form relations? What is the learner's sense of self-efficacy or confidence in his or her skills to attain the criteria of success, and does the learner have the conscientiousness to continue to learn so that he or she reaches this success?

This gives us a selection of factors that can serve as a starting point for developing the mindframe "I focus on learning and the language of learning." The selection is based on evidence but is not intended to be exhaustive.

The next step in developing the mindframe "I focus on learning and the language of learning" is to integrate the methods described earlier for evaluating your students' prior knowledge and experiences into your instruction. In doing so, keep in mind the following finding from empirical educational research: In most classes, learners already know 50 percent of the learning material they are presented by teachers (Nuthall, 2007). Without wishing to reduce teaching to a purely utilitarian activity, but with an eye to accepting responsibility for school learning – we need to break with this waste of learning time. It is critical to gauge the prior knowledge and experiences of your students at the beginning of a teaching sequence, perhaps to develop a concept map after the first learning phase, and make the criteria of success transparent to the students near the beginning of a sequence of lessons.

CHECKLIST

Reflect on the following points next time you plan a lesson:

- Consider the unistructural, multistructural, relational and extended abstract levels.
- Pay attention to the self-efficacy beliefs of your learners.
- Try to assess your students' motivation.
- Get an idea of the way your students work in challenging situations, especially their conscientiousness.
- Try to prevent cognitive overload by avoiding unstructured lessons consisting of vague assignments and confusing worksheets and illustrations on the chalkboard.
- Take care in all phases of your lesson, especially those involving independent activity, to avoid setting the level of challenge too high or too low and intervene cautiously if you observe that this is the case.

EXERCISES

- Go back to the questionnaire for self-reflection at the start of the chapter and complete it again in another color. Where and, more important, why has your perspective on the statements changed? Discuss your self-assessment with a colleague.
- Analyze the initial learning level of your students in regard to achievement, self-efficacy beliefs, motivation, and conscientiousness. Discuss your analysis with a colleague who is familiar with your class.
- Use your analysis of initial learning level when planning your next lesson and make a concept map. Discuss your plan and how you aim to execute it with a colleague.

Visible Learning

A vision

TAYLOR SWIFT & CO. OR HOW TO INSPIRE PASSION FOR LEARNING

I visited the International German School in Brussels in March 2015. After a very stimulating and very pleasant continuing education course, I had a few hours to kill before my flight back to Munich was due to depart. I decided to go to the city center, do some people watching, and enjoy the spring sun. I sat down on a bench in front of the opera house. It was not long before three girls caught my attention and I made the following observation, which left a lasting impression on me: These three girls, who must have been around 13 to 15 years old, were trying to imitate the dance moves Taylor Swift performs in the video to her song "Shake It Off." It was impressive to see how the three girls exerted themselves, how they tried again and again to get a little further into the song, with what intensity they discussed and practiced the moves, copying and correcting each other, how they took mistakes as an opportunity, and – last, but not least – how much fun they had doing it. Learning was visible in these moments. An hour flew by as I watched, and I left for the airport as the three girls continued to practice. I asked myself: Why can't school be like this?

The key thing about this observation is not what the three girls did. Much more impressive is how and why they did what they did. And this brings us back to the main message of this book: Success is based not only on competencies but more on mindframes; less on what we do and more on how we think about what we do. Although there is no denying the significance of competencies, without the corresponding mindframes, they often remain hidden or come to light only in limited form.

There is a quote we have often used in the past that we see as capturing very nicely what it takes to make school and instruction successful. It is from Michael Jordan, one of the most successful basketball players of all time, and is from a commercial that can be viewed on YouTube. We would like to take this quote as the main theme for the conclusion to this book: "I've missed more than 9,000 shots in my career. I've lost almost 300 games. Twenty-six times, I've been trusted to take the game-winning shot and missed. I've failed over and over and over again in my life, and that is why I succeed."

Learning from nature: the web model

There are many books on successful teaching. Two that have enriched the field of German-language pedagogical and educational literature in the past years are Hilbert Meyer's criteria for good teaching (Meyer, 2013) and Andreas Helmke's features of good teaching (Helmke, 2010) – both are no doubt already among the classics in this field. There are many similarly profound books in English, like Thomas Good and Jere Brophy's (2007) *Looking in Classrooms* or Geoff Petty's (2014) *Evidence Based Teaching*. They include many criteria or features of good teaching. In our book, we also include ten mindframes.

If one works on the assumption that the criteria described by Meyer (2013), Helmke (2010), Good and Brophy (2007), or Petty (2014) form a kind of sequential list whose items can be worked through one by one and added to one's repertoire, then our book follows a different understanding of educational expertise. While these authors offer much more than ten points, tips, and tricks, they too form a higher level thinking perspective. The point is not to work through a list on the way to becoming an educational expert – and many have made this mistake when reading *Visible Learning* (ticking off the top ten, and not doing the bottom ten). Rather, the ideas presented in our book form a complete whole, an entirety, a worldview, and we would thus like to characterize them by evoking the image of a web – fully aware that images reduce the complexity of the issues at hand and can thus obscure certain aspects. Still, an image says more than a thousand words and can help to clarify the issues dealt with

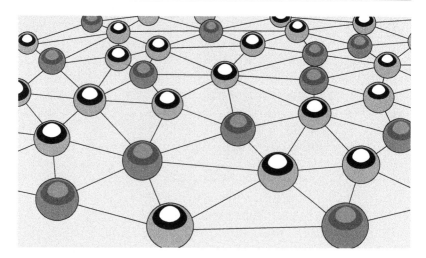

FIGURE 11.1 The web model 1

in this book. Therefore, we are presenting it not at the start of the book but at the end – at the point where you as the reader have already taken the trouble of working through it chapter by chapter (see Figure 11.1).

Webs in general are known for their great durability and for being able to compensate for weak points through the strength of the whole – requiring only a minimum of material to do so. Spiderwebs are particularly interesting in this connection. Researchers have recently discovered that spiders create some of the strongest webs of all, and spider webs are, therefore, now being used as models for artificial webs in many different fields (see Figure 11.2) (Cranford et al., 2012).

What is the secret of spiderwebs? The strength of a spiderweb depends on two factors: First, it depends on the nature of the threads. If the threads are resilient and resistant to tearing, they will form a strong web. Second, the strength of a spiderweb depends on the structure. It can be more stable or unstable depending on the distribution and arrangement of the threads and openings. When these two factors come together, they reinforce each other's influence and balance out each other's weaknesses – remaining stable or returning to a stable state even when a gust of wind rips a hole into them. This characteristic of the web is vital for the spider, because it takes less time and energy to fix a hole than to spin a new web.

If we apply this model to this book and the ideas it contains, then the ten mindframes are the threads that make up the web: The

FIGURE 11.2 The web model 2

stronger they are, the greater their influence on the thinking and actions of teachers will be. At the same time, they are in a reciprocal relationship with each other. If this relationship is loose, there will be a lack of coherency – the mindframes will then be more like patchwork than a unified whole. If, on the other hand, they support and strengthen each other, then the mindframes will form a coherent structure and thus a stable web together. Once again, the whole will be greater than the sum of its parts.

As a result, every mindframe relates to the others, every mindframe results from the others, every mindframe is in a reciprocal relationship with the others, and every mindframe is supported and strengthened by the others. The demands are high, because it is necessary to consider all the mind frames. However, this also leads to the necessary coherency in educational contexts: It is essentially a matter of logic, sound, and consistent thinking and action in situations marked by uncertainty, unpredictability, and often dichotomy. The mindframes discussed in this book should thus not be understood as individual characteristics, as a gift that some people seem to have been given at birth. Rather, they are an expression of educational professionalism, they can be taught and learned, and they form the basis of how high impact teachers think and make the moment-by-moment decisions and judgments in busy, buzzy, and bountiful classrooms.

Visible teaching: making lesson planning visible

Although it is not possible to plan every single aspect of education and instruction, and moments of uncertainty are part of the process, teachers cannot avoid lesson planning – even if not written. One common objection is that we do not know whether lesson planning really helps students to learn more successfully. This then leads to the planning process itself being called into question and to the demand that we focus on the learning rather than the teaching. But in whatever form, planning lessons is critical. At minimum, knowing the nature of the "impact" you want to have on students in a lesson or series of lessons is the core essence of successful planning. We call this "impact" success criteria and tailoring them so that they are based on what students already know and now know, monitoring the progress of all students from this basis toward the criteria of success takes planning – and then this is where the mindframes come into their own – it is the thinking and judgment by the expert (the teacher, and also where it can happen by the student) to know where each student is in the learning cycle toward success, making the adjustments and offering different ways of teaching in the moment that is the core of the art and science of teaching.

Good planning increases the probability that teaching will lead to learning. This may be illustrated by the factor "goals": The more clarity teachers have in regard to their goals (first to themselves and then with the students), the more likely learning will be successful; the better these goals are adjusted to what the learners already know and can do, the more likely learning will be successful; the more they are shared and understood with students, the greater the likelihood that teachers and students will work toward these goals; and the more teachers succeed in reaching an understanding of the goals with the learners, the more likely learning will be successful (and enjoyed). This alone demonstrates the necessity of lesson planning.

The importance of planning is no different for school leaders or for system leaders. Knowing the current situation, having excellent diagnoses, articulating the criteria of success, and then choosing high probability intervention and continually evaluating the success moving from the current state to the desired criteria of success, and frequently smelling the roses of the success of this journey is the essence of good teaching and good system development.

The major message from the research from Visible Learning is that the various influences reflect what *has* happened and should be considered as probability statements. Research is about the past – it sums what *has* happened. Like driving a car, it is worth it to continually pay attention to what is behind you to help best move forward. In a similar manner, it pays to use ideas and methods that have been shown to work systemically. If you introduce a high probability program then there is a higher probability it will have a high effect. It is wise to choose high probability influences. But the key notion is the next step – to "know thy impact": What is the impact in your class or school when you introduce these high probability interventions?

This begs three core questions: What is impact? How would we know we are having an impact? What is a sufficient magnitude of impact? Often, there is no one answer to "what is impact," and we use many such as growth in achievement, feeling of belonging to this place where we learn, wanting to reinvest in more learning, having positive attitudes to the content, willingness to explore what we know and do now know with others, developing curiosity and critical thinking about what we are learning, esteeming respect of self and respect for others, and building confidence to take on more challenges. There are many sources to evaluate what we mean by impact, such as evaluating the will and thrill in learning, observing and listening to students thinking aloud, using test scores to see both growth and attainment, having others observe the impact you are having on students, and exploring artifacts of student work. To evaluate the magnitude, we can use moderation with others, reference to normative growth and attainment criteria, interviews or listening to feelings of belonging in the learning environment, artifacts of student work over time or referenced to an agreed rubric, using assessments to triangulate our beliefs about impact and, most important, providing opportunities for students to know this impact and validating their and your views about their judgments of growth. For each question, there is no one answer – it is a series of triangulated judgments, checked with students and colleagues, hence the importance and power of collective efficacy that all can learn provided this efficacy is fed with evidence of impact.

In many ways, our argument feeds on the motive why most of us entered the education profession: to have a positive impact on the learning lives of students. The core mindframe "I am an evaluator of my impact on student learning" is merely this highlighted. This can be accomplished with the mindframes that we use assessment information to help us understand our impact and that we collaborate with others to critique and moderate our beliefs about what impact means and the magnitude of our impact. We must believe we can change and enhance the learning lives of our students, we must strive to meet this challenge and see potential in students that they may not even see in themselves, we need to teach students to listen and receive our feedback and for us to listen and receive feedback about our impact, and this requires us to listen, to engage in dialogue about learning, to know, respect, and inform them of appropriately challenging criteria of successful learning, to have a deep understanding of the learning cycle, and build all this on high levels of trust and relationship so that it is safe to learn in the environment you are working in. The same applies when considered from the perspective of school leaders in the staffroom and of systems leaders across a system.

Our vision of a school for the future

And, yet, our vision has little to do with the plans so often proposed for reforming the educational system: Reformers too often propose more resources, more autonomy, more international competition, better comparative studies, more statistics, innovative technology, and much more as a sure means of revolutionizing school and instruction. But these measures will not lead to a revolution (see Hattie, 2015). It is not the plans, not the numbers, and not the facts that spark revolutions. People spark revolutions – through their visions, their beliefs, and through their dreams.

Educators continually make competing claims that it is x or y that truly makes the difference, accountability, higher standards, and different forms of schools. Beware of educators with solutions. Education is full of strategies, plans, laws, and mission statements. Martin Luther King Jr did not proclaim "I have a strategy" or "I have a plan"; instead, he said, "I have a dream."

We, too, have a dream for developing passion in learning and developing an education system that values inviting all students to come and learn, to belong, and to reinvest in their own learning.

We have a dream for an education system that develops respect for self and respect for others, to have sensitivity to collaborate with others in the pursuit of learning – no matter white, black, Hispanic, local, refugee, struggling, bright, or other.

We have a dream for an education system peopled by those who want to improve, who want to esteem excellence, who want to know progress, and who know what to do when they do not know what to do.

We have a dream for teachers and school leaders to be respected and valued, both in societal and in financial terms. Who see themselves and whom we also see as the major change agents in student learning – thus demonstrating the law and the faith we have in schools to truly make a difference to our society. Surely the greatest civilizing institution in our democracy is our schools.

We have a dream for students to be taught to have confidence to want to take on challenges, to say "this is hard and I want to try," not "this is hard I cannot do it."

We have a dream to get rid of those things that do not work, to get rid of so much stuff we try to implant in kids' heads, to find the balance of surface to deep to transfer in a fun and joyful way that means our students want to belong, to come back and learn more.

1. The purpose of education:

   ■ We want all students to learn precious and productive knowledge – to critique, reorganize, disrupt, and celebrate this knowledge and to learn what they would not learn if they did not come to school.

   The purpose of education should never be to meet the needs of children; what a lowly aspiration this is that help keep kids in their place – the rich man in the castle, the poor boy and girl at the gate. The purpose of education should not be to help students reach their potential, as again this lowers the aspirations for many and defeats the purpose of schooling. The *prime* purpose of education is to help students exceed what they think is their potential. To see in students something they may not see in themselves and to imbue them with our passion for learning.

2. We are living our dream:

   ■ But we are living our dream – as there is so much success around us right NOW. Unlike Martin Luther King Jr's claim that still there is no freedom for his peoples, those who are young in our society, those who come to our shores (seeking countries with great schooling systems) have access to a system of schooling that does have many oases of excellence.

- We do have teachers and schools that teach children how to cash the check to Life and share the Liberty and the pursuit of Happiness while they are still children.

- Our job is to locate these havens of hope and invite others to be like them.

- We see evidence of so many students privileged to be with such teachers and already living the dream. We see teachers who want to share the passion of their knowledge; who privilege progress leading to achievement; who know when to move from surface to deep and back again; who know deeply how to enhance the learning lives of their students; who have the social sensitivities to know how to interact with colleagues to sharpen, enhance, share, and enjoy their expertise in having a profound impact on their students.

3. We have much to do:

- But we do have much to do; we often still have an education system based on Pollyanna claims that does not offer excellence for all. There are still too many vicious inequalities, too much deficit thinking, too little trust in expertise, too many witch hunts, and not enough treasure hunts.

- But there is excellence around us – have we the spine, the courage to dependably identify these schools, leaders, and teachers that are making major changes to the learning lives of their students, build coalitions of success around these educators, and then support collaborative communities of such excellence within and between schools?

- There are many schools, Visible Learning schools and others, experiencing this success every day and they are living our dreams.

- This is our dream for education that I want for our children and grandchildren, and for every child to experience. Know thy impact, spark the learning, and let us all live the dream.

Bibliography

Adey, P., & Shayer, M. (2013). Piagetian approaches. In J.A.C. Hattie & E. Anderman (Eds.) *Handbook on student achievement*. New York: Routledge.

Adey, P., Shayer, M., & Yates, C. (2001). *Thinking science: The curriculum materials of the CASE project* (3rd edn). London: Nelson Thornes.

Alexander, R. J., & Armstrong, M. (2010). *Children, their world, their education: Final report and recommendations of the Cambridge Primary Review*. New York: Taylor & Francis.

Aristotle, U. (2004). *Rhetoric*. Whitefish, MT: Kessinger Publishing.

Berliner, D. C. (1988). *The development of expertise in pedagogy*. Washington, DC: AACTE Publications.

Biggs, J., & Collis, K. (1982). *Evaluating the quality of learning: The SOLO taxonomy*. New York: Academic Press.

Bloom, B. (1984). *Taxonomy of educational objectives (1956)*. New York: Pearson Education.

Bollnow, O. F. (2001). Die pädagogische Atmosphäre. Untersuchungen über die gefühlsmäßigen zwischenmenschlichen Voraussetzungen der Erziehung. Essen: Die blaue Eule 2001 (1968).

Bolton, S., & Hattie, J. A. C. (in review). *Development of the brain, executive functioning and Piaget*.

Brookhart, S. M. (2017). *How to give effective feedback to your students*. Alexandria, VA: ASCD.

Brophy, J. E. (1999). *Teaching* (pp. 8–9). New York: International Academy of Education and the International Bureau of Education.

Buber, M. (1958). *Ich und Du*. Heidelberg: Lambert Schneider.

Clinton, J., Cairns, K., Mclaren, P., & Simpson, S. (2014). Evaluation of the Victorian Deaf Education Institute Real-Time Captioning Pilot Program, Final Report – August 2014. The University of Melbourne: Centre for Program Evaluation.

Coe, R. (2012). Effect size. In *Research methods and methodologies in education*, Arthur, J., Waring, M., Coe, R. & Hedges, L.V. (eds). Thousand Oaks, CA: Sage Publishing, 368–377.

Cranford, S. W., Tarakanova, A., Pugno, N. M., & Buehler, M. J. (2012). Nonlinear material behaviour of spider silk yields robust webs. *Nature, 482*, 72–76.

Csíkszentmihályi, M. (2008). *Flow: The psychology of optimal experience.* New York: Harper.

Dewey, J. (2009). *Democracy and education: An introduction to the philosophy of education.* Seattle, WA: CreateSpace.

Donoghue, G., & Hattie, J. A. C. (in review). Learning strategies: A meta-analysis of Dunlosky et al. (2013).

Dweck, C. (2012). *Mindset: How you can fulfill your potential.* New York: Random House.

Dweck, C. (2015). Carol Dweck revisits the 'growth mindset'. *Education Week, 35*(5), 20–24.

Dweck, C. (2017). *Mindset: Changing the way you think to fulfil your potential.* New York: Hachette.

Eells, R. (2011). Meta-analysis of the relationship between collective efficacy and student achievement. Unpublished Ph.D dissertation. Loyola University of Chicago.

Endres, A., & Martiensen, J. (2007). *Mikroökonomik – Eine integrierte Darstellung traditioneller Praxis und moderner Konzepte in Theorie und Praxis.* Stuttgart: Kohlhammer.

Fishbein, M., & Ajzen, I. (1975). *Belief, attitude, intention, and behavior.* Reading, MA: Addison-Wesley.

Fisher, D., Frey, N., & Farnan, N. (2004). Student teachers matter: The impact of student teachers on elementary-aged children in a professional development school. *Teacher Education Quarterly, 31*(2), 43–56.

Flanders, N. A. (1970). *Analyzing teacher behavior* (pp. 100–107). Boston, MA: Addison-Wesley P. C.

Friere, P. (2000). *Pedagogy of the oppressed.* London: Bloomsbury Publishing.

Gan, J. S. M. (2011). The effects of prompts and explicit coaching on peer feedback quality. Unpublished PhD dissertation. University of Auckland.

Gardner, H., Csíkszentmihályi, M., & Damon, W. (2001). *Good work: When excellence and ethics meet.* Zus. mit Howard Gardner and William Damon. New York: Basic Books.

Gardner, H., Csíkszentmihályi, M., & Damon, W. (2005). *Good work.* Stuttgart: Klett.

Good, T. L., & Brophy, J. E. (2007). *Looking in classrooms* (10th edn). London: Pearson.

Guskey, T. R. (2010). Lessons of mastery learning. *Educational Leadership, 68*(2), 52.

Haimovitz, K., & Dweck, C. S. (2016). What predicts children's fixed and growth intelligence mind-sets? Not their parents' views of intelligence but their parents' views of failure. *Psychological Science,* 0956797616639727.

Hattie, J. (2009). *Visible learning.* London: Routledge.

Hattie, J. (2012). *Visible learning for teachers.* London: Routledge.

Hattie, J. (2013). *Lernen sichtbar machen.* Baltmannsweiler: Schneider.

Hattie, J. (2014). *Lernen sichtbar machen für Lehrpersonen.* Baltmannsweiler: Schneider.

Hattie, J. (2015). *Lernen sichtbar machen aus psychologischer Perspektive.* Baltmannsweiler: Schneider.

Hattie, J., & Masters, D. (2011). *The evaluation of a student feedback survey.* Auckland: Cognition.

Hattie, J., & Timperley, H. (2007). The power of feedback. *Review of Educational Research*, 77(1), 81–112.

Hattie, J., & Yates, G. (2015). *Visible learning and the science of how we learn*. New York: Routledge.

Hattie, J., & Zierer, K. (2017). Kenne deinen Einfluss! "Visible Learning" für die Unterrichtspraxis. Baltmannsweiler: Schneider.

Hattie, J. (1992). *Self-concept*. Hillsdale, NJ: Lawrence Erlbaum Associates.

Hattie, J., & Donoghue, G. (2016). Learning strategies: A synthesis and conceptual model. *Nature: Science of Learning, 1*. doi:10.1038/npjscilearn.2016.13. www.nature.com/articles/npjscilearn201613

Helmke, A. (2010). *Unterrichtsqualität und Lehrerprofessionalität. Diagnose, Evaluation und Verbesserung des Unterrichts*. Stuttgart: Klett.

Herbart, J.-F. (1808). *Allgemeine Pädagogik aus dem Zweck der Erziehung abgeleitet*. Bochum: Kamp.

Keller, J. (2010). *Motivational design for learning and performance*. The ARCS Model Approach. London: Springer.

Kiel, E., Keller-Schneider, M., Haag, L., & Zierer, K. (2014). *Unterricht planen, durchführen, reflektieren*. Berlin: Cornelsen.

King, Martin L., Jr. (1963). "I Have a Dream." Speech. Lincoln Memorial, Washington, D. C. 28 Aug. 1963.

Klafki, W. (1996). *Neue Studien zur Bildungstheorie und Didaktik – Zeitgemäße Allgemeinbildung und kritisch-konstruktive Didaktik, 5., unveränderte Auflage*. Weinheim/Basel: Beltz.

Korpershoek, H., Harms, T., de Boer, H., van Kuijk, M., & Doolaard, S. (2016). A meta-analysis of the effects of classroom management strategies and classroom management programs on students' academic, behavioral, emotional, and motivational outcomes. *Review of Educational Research, 86*(3).

Lipsey, M., & Wilson, D. (2001). *Practical meta-analysis*. Thousand Oaks, CA: Sage.

Littleton, K., Mercer, N., Dawes, L., Wegerif, R., Rowe, D., & Sams, C. (2005). Talking and thinking together at key stage 1. *Early Years, 25*(2), 167–182.

Lomas, J. D., Koedinger, K., Patel, N., Shodhan, S., Poonwala, N., & Forlizzi, J. L. (2017, May). Is Difficulty Overrated?: The Effects of Choice, Novelty and Suspense on Intrinsic Motivation in Educational Games. In *Proceedings of the 2017 CHI Conference on Human Factors in Computing Systems* (pp. 1028–1039). Denver, CO: ACM.

Mager, R. (1997). *Preparing instructional objectives: A critical tool in the effective performance*. London: Kogan Page.

Martin, A. J. (2012). The role of personal best (PB) goals in the achievement and behavioral engagement of students with ADHD and students without ADHD. *Contemporary Educational Psychology, 37*(2), 91–105.

Martin, A. J., Collie, R. J., Mok, M., & McInerney, D. M. (2016). Personal best (PB) goal structure, individual PB goals, engagement, and achievement: A study of Chinese-and English-speaking background students in Australian schools. *British Journal of Educational Psychology, 86*(1), 75–91.

Merrill, M. D. (2002). First principles of instruction. *Educational Technology Research and Development, 50*(3), 43–59.

Mesmer-Magnus, J., Glew, D. J., & Viswesvaran, C. (2012). A meta-analysis of positive humor in the workplace. *Journal of Managerial Psychology, 27*(2), 155–190.

MET (2010). Learning about Teaching. Bill & Melinda Gates Foundation.

Meyer, H. L. (2013). *Was ist guter Unterricht?* (9. Aufl.). Berlin: Cornelsen Scriptor.

Mischel, W. (2014). *The Marshmallow test: Mastering self-control.* New York: Little Brown.

Mitchell, D. (2014). *What really works in special and inclusive education: Using evidence-based teaching strategies.* New York: Routledge.

Murphy, M. C., & Dweck, C. S. (2016). Mindsets shape consumer behavior. *Journal of Consumer Psychology, 26*(1), 127–136.

Nohl, H. (1970). *Die pädagogische Bewegung in Deutschland und ihre Theorie. 7. Auflage.* Frankfurt a.M.: Schulte-Bulmke.

Norton, M. I., Mochon, D., & Ariely, D. (2012). The IKEA effect: When labor leads to love. *Journal of Consumer Psychology, 22*(3) (July), 453–460.

Nuthall, G. A. (2007). *The hidden lives of learners.* Wellington: New Zealand Council for Educational Research.

Nystrand, M. (1997). *Opening dialogue: Understanding the dynamics of language and learning in the English classroom.* New York: Teachers College Press.

Paas, F. G., & Van Merriënboer, J. J. (1994). Variability of worked examples and transfer of geometrical problem-solving skills: A cognitive-load approach. *Journal of Educational Psychology, 86*(1), 122.

Petty, G. (2014). *Evidence based teaching.* Oxford: Oxford University Press.

Ridley, M. (2010). *The rational optimist: How prosperity evolves.* New York: Harper Perennial.

Rubie-Davies, C. (2014). *Becoming a high expectation teacher: Raising the bar.* London: Routledge.

Rubie-Davies, C. (2016). *High and low expectation teachers.* Interpersonal and Intrapersonal Expectancies, 145.

Rutter, M., Maughan, B., Mortimore, P., & Ouston, J. (1980). *15 000 Stunden: Schulen und ihre Wirkung auf die Kinder.* Basel: Weinheim/Basel.

Scriven, M. (1967). The methodology of evaluation. In R. W. Tyler, R. M. Gagne, & M. Scriven (Eds.) *Perspectives of curriculum evaluation,* pp. 39–83. AERA Monograph Series on Curriculum Evaluation, 1. Chicago, IL: Rand McNally.

Shayer, M. (1999). Cognitive acceleration through science education II: Its effects and scope. *International Journal of Science Education, 21*(8), 883–902.

Shayer, M., & Adey, P. S. (1981). *Towards a science of science teaching.* London: Heinemann Educational Books.

Shayer, M., & Adey, P. S. (1993). Accelerating the development of formal thinking in middle and high school students IV: Three years after a two-year intervention. *Journal of Research in Science Teaching, 30*(4), 351–366.

Sinek, S. (2009). *Start with why: How great leaders inspire everyone to take action.* New York: Penguin.

Snook, I., O'Neill, J., Clark, J., O'Neill, A. M., & Openshaw, R. (2009). Invisible learnings? A commentary on John Hattie's book: Visible learning: A synthesis of over 800 meta-analyses relating to achievement. *New Zealand Journal of Educational Studies, 44*(1), 93.

Van den Bergh, L., Ros, A., & Beijaard, D. (2010). Feedback van basisschoolleerkrachten tijdens actief leren. de huidige praktijk. ORD-paper. ORD: Enschede.

Wernke, S., & Zierer, K. (2016). Lehrer als Eklektiker!? 58 Grundzüge einer Eklektischen Didaktik. *Friedrich Jahresheft "Lehren"*.

Wiliam, D., & Leahy, S. (2015). *Embedding formative assessment: Practical techniques for F-12 classrooms*. Cheltenham, VIC: Hawker Brownlow Education.

Yeager, D. S., & Dweck, C. S. (2012). Mindsets that promote resilience: When students believe that personal characteristics can be developed. *Educational Psychologist, 47*(4), 302–314.

Young, M. (2013). Overcoming the crisis in curriculum theory: A knowledge-based approach. *Journal of Curriculum Studies, 45*(2), 101–118.

Zhu, X., & Simon, H. A. (1987). Learning mathematics from examples and by doing. *Cognition and Instruction, 4*(3), 137–166.

Zierer, K. (2016a). Alles eine Frage der Technik? Erfolgreiches Lehren als Symbiose von Kompetenz und Haltung. *Friedrich Jahresheft "Lehren"*.

Zierer, K. (2016b). *Hattie für gestresste Lehrer. Kernbotschaften und Handlungsempfehlungen aus John Hatties "Visible Learning" und "Visible Learning for Teachers"*. Baltmannsweiler: Schneider.

Index

Boldface page references indicate boxed text. *Italic* references indicate figures.